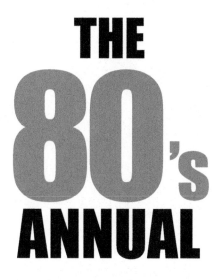

THE 80's ANNUAL

by
SARAH LEWIS

First Edition
Published 2016
NEW HAVEN PUBLISHING LTD
www.newhavenpublishingltd.com
newhavenpublishing@gmail.com

Interior and cover design © Pete Cunliffe
pcunliffe@blueyonder.co.uk

newhaven
publishing

Welcome to The 80's Annual,

a collection of features, photos and fun for the adult child of the Eighties. Anyone who remembers the excitement of receiving an annual as a Christmas present, will enjoy the nostalgic familiarity of The 80's Annual, as well as uncovering new discoveries about some of their favourite faces of the decade.

Including a year-by-year retrospective look at the fads, fashions, highlights and events of the Eighties, puzzles, word searches, fiction, celebrity interviews, festival reviews and more, there really is something for everyone who is part of the generation who grew up sticking tape over the broken tabs on cassettes, so they could be used for re-recording.

Whether you are a die-hard music fan or simply love the Eighties, whether you're a 'flicker' or methodically make your way through from cover to cover, you will enjoy all this annual has to offer. If you want to know the worst 80's fashion mistakes made by John Parr, Paul Hardcastle and Jay Aston, discover how Phil Fearon nearly became a member of the Sex Pistols, read interviews with Bruce Foxton, The Selecter and Johnny Hates Jazz, or simply test how much of the decade you can remember in one of the 80's quizzes, you will find it all and much, much more here.

So, put the Betamax on pause, grab a can of Tab and a Texan bar, and get ready to ride on time. Going back to the Eighties has never been so much fun!

In Conversation with
The Selecter

As we entered the Eighties, The Selecter were riding the wave of success brought by the release of 'On My Radio' at the end of 1979. A year of increasing popularity for Ska and Two-Tone music, 1980 saw the band continue their strong chart presence with the singles 'Three Minute Hero', 'Missing Words' and 'The Whisper'. The band's split in 1982 saw lead singer Pauline Black embark on an acting and presenting career. Reforming in 1991, The Selecter toured and recorded for a further 15 years, before taking a break for the singer to write her autobiography 'Black By Design'. Returning to performing and to the studio in 2009, along with original band member Arthur 'Gaps' Hendrickson, The Selecter continue to release new material and feature on the retro festival scene, as well as the band's own long list of gigs.

This year, Pauline Black and Gaps Hendrickson joined Jools Holland's Rhythm and Blues Orchestra's UK tour. I caught up with the pair in April, ahead of their performance at Margate's Winter Gardens, to talk about music, racism and keeping the message of Two-Tone alive.

Why do you think Two-Tone and Ska music have remained so popular?

Gaps: "It surprises all of us. After all this time, it's a privilege to be able to do the music we love."

Pauline: "I've always thought that the Two-Tone Movement was a far greater thing, and a better thing in some ways, than all the little bands that were involved in it. Together we had strength, that's what I thought. I still think it would be really, really great if everybody came back together and did one big, huge gig somewhere, just to underline the fact we still believe that, and we still believe Two-Tone has a place in this world and still has something to say about the conditions a lot of people have to live under."

Do you feel there is less pressure in writing and performing now compared to in the Eighties?

Pauline: "I think you have to set yourself goals. Gaps and I, when we first got the band into shape again in 2010, each year has had a goal. Each of the last three years, we've pretty much had a new album and tours, taking it not just UK but doing America and Australia, making that circle wider."

Gaps: "The pressure at the beginning was different to pressure now."

Pauline: "Too Much Pressure!"

Gaps: "We can be more creative [now]."

Pauline: "As long as the books balance at the end of the year, then that's fine. More bands go under from getting their finances wrong, or doing business wrong, those kind of things than they do probably from not having creative spirit. There's lots of creative bands out there. It's quite difficult to use what you have, especially when you're a band like us, which has a heritage that people know and like, and you're trying to do something new as well. We seem to have steered a bit of a path through that."

Do you think that is because you now manage The Selecter?

Pauline: "Well, in conjunction with them [the band]. I wouldn't say it's a democracy, but it's a very sort of benign autocracy." [Pauline and Gaps laugh]. "I do canvass opinion."

You both perform with an incredible energy on stage. Is that because you're still singing with passion and belief?

Pauline: "That, and I think we actually like each other."

Gaps: "More so now, probably."

Pauline: "There are still loads of things to talk about, which fit into what the original remit was of the original Selecter, which was to push the whole thing of Two-Tone. Black people, white people in the same band, working together towards the same end, highlighting racism and sexism. Well, none of that's really gone away, has it? In fact, there's quite a few more 'isms' there now, that you couldn't talk about then but you can now."

I read that you encountered racism during your first tour of America in 1980. What happened when you arrived in Texas?

Pauline: "We all went to the Southfork Ranch and posed for some photos for Sounds magazine. People who'd let their necks redden in the sun, they turned up in a flat-bed truck with baseball bats, and suddenly decided there were too many N-words on the fence. Would we mind getting out of there? They didn't actually say that to us. They took our bus driver, who was a bit of a redneck himself, aside to inform us that it was probably better if we got back on the bus. So, back on the bus we got."

Was that your first time abroad?

Gaps: "It was the first time in America."

Pauline: "We did coast to coast. We flew into Vancouver, then went all the way back to New York, all through the South and the rest of it. That took about six weeks, and then we got to New York and they wanted us back in L.A. for two shows a night at the Whisky A Go Go, so we had to fly back to that coast again.

Gaps: "It was good though, two gigs a night."

Pauline: "It was a good experience, yes. We were kind of out there on our own because there were six black people in our band, one white person. In The Specials you've got two black people, so you've got five [white] people kind of protecting them. Madness were all white, so they didn't have at all the kind of problems we had when we went through the South.

We had Juliet [Billy Bragg's wife] managing us. She was just a diminutive, 4ft 11 blonde, and I remember getting off the bus. Our tour manager and all of us going into a truck stop, and the whole place just went dead. We sat there for a bit, didn't get served. We got up and got back on the bus. When you think about it, it was only 10 or 11 years after the assassination of Martin Luther King. You don't reconstitute a redneck into a caring human being, do you?"

How do those experiences compare with society today?

Pauline: "Things have shifted. If you're a racist these days, you get called out. The day-to-day kind of petty racism still goes on, I think, in the same way that the day-to-day petty anti-women nonsense goes on."

Gaps: "People are a bit more mindful now. They respect that racism is still there."

As pioneers of the Two-Tone movement, who are your musical influences?

Pauline: "If I was absolutely honest, I suppose I'd probably say Mick Jagger. Just because of the whole image he puts into a performance. I was always taken with all of the energy he put into a performance. I just thought he was incredible. Also guitarists, people like Jimi Hendrix."

Gaps: "Yes, [he's] just unique."

Pauline: "I should probably choose a woman, I suppose. There's the softer side of me, which is people like Joni Mitchell and Joan Armatrading, 'cause I started out being quite folky really. It was the only way you could get a gig unless you could join a band. What else were you going to do in the mid to late Seventies if you were a woman? Since I joined The Selecter, there's no holding back."

Gaps: "Obviously, a lot of reggae stars. My first influence was Bob Marley. Beyond that though, all the reggae music that comes from Jamaica, and people like The Ethiopians, Steel Pulse and Osibisa. I like Boccherini and

Tchaikovsky. I love the music I'm involved with ... I love all kinds of music. Music is my first love."

Pauline: "I think you have to as well stay in touch with what's going on now. I don't mean sit down and listen to Justin Bieber, but music is music. It doesn't matter how young or old you are, you can appreciate what somebody else does."

How does performing with Jools Holland compare with a Selecter gig?

Pauline: "Well, it's different because we have to fit in, if you see what I mean. We've been invited along to come and do something. They're very generously sharing their viewpoint on some of our songs, and collaboratively, we kind of get it together. Gaps and I put a lot of energy into our show that we do with The Selecter. Coming along and doing five songs with Jools ... physically it's a lot easier, but nonetheless going on to a cold audience, an audience who's there to listen to maybe an R&B orchestra, and maybe doesn't even know what Ska is. There's some winning over to be done. It's a challenge really. It's worked out, it's great. Jools is so generous of spirit in

terms of all his music making, and all the musicians he works with, that it's an absolute riot, a joy."

What about performing at a retro festival amongst different music genres, when you could be following a group like Bananarama?

Pauline: "We're normally on before them! I think they're lovely ... they've got lovely cardigans. Last time we were there [Rewind] we went on after Kid Creole. I didn't know it was Kid Creole ... he was a love interest from 1981 ... I hadn't seen him since."

Talking of cardigans, I'd like to finish our chat by asking what was your worst fashion faux pas of the Eighties?

Pauline: "The most horrendous fashion faux pas I made was at our first gig. I was wearing pink spandex trousers."

Gaps: "I think mine was a boiler suit."

Pauline: "Yes, like a Clockwork Orange sort of boiler suit."

Read more from this interview in 'More Eighties', to be published by New Haven Publishing in 2017.

1980 That was the year...

Paul McCartney was arrested

During Wings' tour of Japan, the former member of the Fab Four was arrested on 16th January at Narita International Airport, whilst in possession of 8oz of marijuana. He was released after nine days at Tokyo Narcotics Detention, with no charges filed, as the Japanese government felt he had learnt his lesson. Almost four years to the day later, on 15th January 1984, McCartney and his wife Linda were arrested in Barbados for possessing marijuana. They were released after each paying a $100 fine.

****

Radio Caroline ship sunk

On 19th March, during a storm off the Essex coast, Mi Amigo lost its anchor and began to drift. The crew were rescued by lifeboat 'Helen Turnbull', sent from the Kent town of Sheerness, as the Pirate Radio ship started to take on water. The following day, 19km from where it had originally been anchored, the broadcasting vessel sunk.

****

Who Shot J.R.?

There was worldwide speculation as to who shot Larry Hagman's character J. R. Ewing, in the American soap "Dallas". It became commonplace to see T-shirts bearing the slogan "I Shot J.R.". The phrase was also used as the title of a single by The Wurzels. The public were finally put out of their misery in November, when Kristin Shephard (played by Mary Crosby) was revealed as the culprit.

****

Iranian Embassy Siege

On 30th April, 26 people were taken hostage by opponents of Ayatollah Khomeini, at the Iranian Embassy in South Kensington, London. Following the shooting of one of the hostages on 5th May, the SAS stormed the building, killing five of the six terrorists. The remaining terrorist, Fowzi Nejad, was sentenced to life imprisonment.

****

Pac-Man launched

Released in Japan on 22nd May, the Namco arcade game went on to become the best-selling game of all time.

****

Björn Borg won his 5th Wimbledon title

On 6th July, the Swede successfully defended his title against John McEnroe, to win the Men's Singles for the fifth consecutive year. It was also to be Borg's final year as Wimbledon Champion.

****

Summer Olympic Games are held in Moscow

Taking place between 19th July and 3rd August, this was the first time the event had been held in a Communist country. The Soviet war in Afghanistan led to 65 countries, including the U.S.A., Japan and West Germany, boycotting the games. This prompted a retaliatory USSR-led boycott, by 14 Eastern Bloc countries, of the 1984 Summer Olympics in Los Angeles.

****

Lech Walesa led Solidarity in Poland

On 14th August, following further food price rises, workers staged a walkout at the Lenin Shipyard in Gdansk. It inspired further strikes throughout Poland which, under Walesa's leadership, were co-ordinated by Solidarity. On 8th October 1982, the Polish government banned all Trade Unions, including Solidarity, forcing Walesa to continue his work underground. He was awarded the Nobel Peace Prize for his efforts in 1983.

****

John Lennon shot dead

Returning home to The Dakota building in New York on 8th December, Lennon was fatally wounded when Mark Chapman fired five shots at the former Beatle.

****
We said a final goodbye to:

Alfred Hitchcock, Billy Butlin, Bon Scott, Colonel Sanders, Hattie Jacques, Ian Curtis, Jesse Owens, John Bonham, Mae West, Peter Sellers, Steve McQueen and Yootha Joyce.

****
UK Chart Toppers included:

Pink Floyd
- Another Brick In The Wall

Blondie
- Atomic, Call Me, and The Tide Is High

The Jam
- Going Underground and Start

Kenny Rogers
- Coward of The County

Johnny Logan
- What's Another Year

Abba
- The Winner Takes It All and Super Trouper.

****
Top Films included:

Airplane, The Empire Strikes Back, 9 to 5, Flash Gordon, American Gigolo, Xanadu, The Blue Lagoon, The Shining, Raging Bull and The Blues Brothers.

****
Rear of The Year:

The competition had yet to be established as an annual event, but had it been judged this year, it would probably have been won by Sheena Easton!

80's MUSIC

ACROSS

1 and 2 down, 44 across Madness single released in January 1981 (3,6,2,3,3,6,5)

2 Music show hosted by Alistair Pirrie (10)

7 and 13 down, 36 across Special AKA's protest song of 1984 (4,6,7)

11 Renate Blauel's ex-husband (5,4)

14 He sang the opening line of Band Aid's "Do They Know It's Christmas" (4,5)

15 See 15 down

16 and 34 down Alyson Williams' 1989 Top 10 hit (5,4)

17 Didn't Whitney almost have it? (3)

18 Starlight's number? (3)

19 and 32 across Initially, Wang Chung sang about doing this in L.A. in 1985 (1,1,1,1)

20 See 15 down

22 Is Paul Weller the father? (3)

23 1987 hit for Mel & Kim (1,1,1)

24 See 4 down

27 Let Me Touch You was the 1987 album from this back-stabbing group (5)

29 Roachford had a cuddly one

30 How Bananarama began to Kiss Him Goodbye "_ , _ , Hey Hey" (2,2)

31 See 24 down

32 See 19 across

34 Initially, Coventry's fun boy will be thinking of you (1,1)

35 and 53 across The Kids From Fame were on this faithful frequency in 1982 (2,8)

36 See 7 across

38 What Godley & Creme wanted to do in 1985 (3)

39 Culture or Timex Social? (4)

40 Michael Jackson album featuring eight Top 20 singles (3)

41 See 21 down

43 What Eric Clapton was behind in 1987 (4)

44 See 1 across

49 This 1989 Top 20 hit for the Lightning Seeds was untainted (4)

50 Where Tiffany liked to perform her songs (4)

53 See 35 across

54 See 32 down

DOWN

1 A hit for Wet, Wet, Wet and Heaven 17 (10)

2 See 1 across

3 Morley, Horn and Sinclair's record label (4,4,4)

4 and 12 down, 24 across Duran Duran had a new one in 1983 (4,2,6)

5 and 28 down He sang the theme from Moonlighting (2,7)

6 Messrs Gibbons, Hill and Beard (1,1,3)

8 Stock, Aitken & Waterman's girls would rather jack (8)

9 They told us to Hold On Tight (1,1,1)

10 Where The Housemartins were hatched (4)

12 See 4 down

13 See 7 across

15 and 15 across, 20 across, 20 down, 33 down, 42 down Song released at the end of 1980 by The Police (2,2,2,2,2,2,2,2)

19 Ms Wilcox shared her name with her band (5)

20 See 15 down

21 and 41 across, 51 down Kool & The Gang Song "Ooh, _ , _ , _" (2,2,2)

22 Wham! sang about being yours in 1985 (3)

24 and 31 across, 50 down Number 2 hit for Slade in 1983 (2,2,2)

25 The hero of Indeep's 1983 Top 20 hit (1,1)

26 "_ Mo Be There" by James Ingram and Michael McDonald (3)

28 See 5 down

32 and 54 across A.K.A. Stuart Goddard (4,3)

33 See 15 down

34 See 16 across

37 Initially, Kajagoogoo's bass player (1,1)

42 See 15 down

44 Ms Arnold performed with The Beatmasters on Burn It Up (1,1)

45 Initially, she duetted with Aaron Neville in 1989 (1,1)

46 Charlene had never been here in 1982 (2)

47 It was all about her for this trio (3)

48 Iron Maiden's record label (1,1,1)

50 See 24 down

51 See 21 down

52 Initially, Haircut 100's bass player (1,1)

MISS YOU LIKE CRAZY

The Eighties may well be alive in our memories and music collections, but some of the things we loved about the decade look destined to be consigned to the past forever:

80's Hair - Okay, so floppy fringes, footballer's perms and mullets may make us cringe now. Sun-In, Wash-In-Wash-Out hair colour and pots of pungent smelling hair gel may not have been the height of sophistication. But at least we all had hair to style as we pleased, and dyed it out of desire rather than necessity.

Sweet Treats - Texan, Banjo, Nutty Bars, Cabana, Treets and Pacers are just a few of the 80's delights our taste buds would love to return to the shops. Summer has never been the same since we lost icy favourites such as Midnight Mint choc ices and Snofrute, Haunted House, King Kong and Heart lollies.

Our Tune - Many a morning tear was shed listening to the feature on Simon Bates' Radio 1 show. Now, the only reason the radio station is likely to make us cry is down to the music it plays.

Spitting Image - Besides entertaining us, the satirical puppet show raised political awareness in a generation of 80's kids.

Being Bored - Constant online accessibility and increasingly busy lifestyles leave little opportunity for the luxury of boredom. Even waiting at the bus stop becomes a chance to catch up with emails.

Ford Escort XR3i - Between the boy racers and hairdressers driving around in them, there was a time when every other car on the road seemed to be this 80's iconic motor. Today, a Classic Car Show is the likeliest place to find one.

World of Sport - Presented by Dickie Davies, the Saturday afternoon TV show brought us an array of sporting coverage including Wrestling and the Results Service, an education in curious-sounding Scottish football teams like Partick Thistle, Stenhousemuir, Queen of The South and Hamilton Academical.

Smash Hits - From lyrics to the latest gossip, the magazine brought us everything relevant to our young lives.

Dictionaries - With a world of information online at our fingertips, today's generation of kids will never know the simple pleasure of looking up rude words in the dictionary. Almost as much fun was punching 5318008 into a calculator, then turning it upside down!

Dressing To Impress - Whether you were a Mod, Punk, New Romantic or head-to-toe in High Street fashion, going out meant making more of an effort than throwing on jeans and a t-shirt. We wanted to see and be seen.

Opinions - Not the mindless nonsense that's bandied about on social media, but the discussions and debates we used to have before apathy and political correctness got a stranglehold on society.

And not forgetting ...

Some of our 80's hairstyles

Top Of The Pops
Woolworths
Ceefax/Teletext
The Young Ones
Blackadder
12" singles
SNOB
C60 & C90 cassettes
Rentaghost
Cans of Top Deck
Jokes on lolly sticks
Tales of The Unexpected
Perfumed rubbers
Clackers
Picture Discs
Athena Posters

The Untrendy Teenager's Thoughts on...
Frankie, Wham! and Duran Duran

The Untrendy Teenager began to post entries on her Secret 80's Diary blog at the beginning of 2016. Here, she shares more of those excerpts.

21st January, 1984
A new group called Frankie Goes to Hollywood is No. 1 with a song called Relax. I've not heard it yet.

26th January
Frankie has been banned from Top of The Pops cos it's dirty apparently. Must listen to it and see what all the fuss is about!

28th January
Listened to Frankie. It's disgusting. It says something like "when you want to lick and chew it" - I love it!

7th February
On the school bus someone told us why Relax is so rude. Apparently the word 'come' means to fiddle with yourself! No wonder it got banned then!!

29th February
Nena is No. 1 - GRRRRR. I have gone off it a bit. I was hoping

Relax would stay there for six weeks and tie with Karma Chameleon, and now Nena has spoiled it. Oh Frankie! Oh Frankie! Oh Frankie!! OH FRANKIE!!!!!

18th April
Wrote furious letter to Blue Suede Views, the Teletext pop mag, because a silly cow said that Duran loved themselves and expected everyone else to too (although I do anyway – Roger!!). She also liked Boy George. I've held my peace so far, but that did it.

26th April
Roger (Taylor) is 24 today. Mmmm great. Happy birthday love. Great day. Saw TOTP. Frankie 29 still. Hello is still No. 1 but I don't mind because Duran's new single The Reflex is a new entry at No. 5. Duran were on TOTP. Janice Long sang Happy Birthday to Roger. He looked gorgeous!

12th June
FRANKIE NO. 1!! With Two Tribes. Straight in too! Relax is also No. 11! D'ran 19. Best chart ever. Bronski Beat No. 4 - FAB! Heard 12" of Two Tribes. It's ACE, I must buy it. I LOVE it!

14th June
Frankie were on TOTP with Two Tribes. Everyone wore shirts saying Relax Don't Do It, etc. I'm looking for one on Saturday. Also buying 12". It was funny as I'd never seen Frankie on TOTP before, and Mike Read was presenting it. Hee, hee! Nick Heyward and Nik Kershaw were on TOTP too. Mum got them mixed up of course. Dad made insulting remarks about them and Frankie.

17th June
Listened to Two Tribes 12" again. Luv it more than ever. B-side too. I

luv Holly again too. Makes me wonder what the 12" of Relax would have been like. Brill, I expect. This is nearly better than Relax. If there's ever a nuclear war it'll remind me of this. Probably be the last record I play. Wrote down all the words to it, which took a long time. ACE MAN!

19th June
Two Tribes is still No. 1, Relax is No 5. Eat your heart out Boy George! Who cares if Holly's gay? Ace singer and sexy with it. Frankie have now had as many No. 1s as Duran and Culture Club. I hope they beat Culture Club but not Duran.

28th June
TOTP was good. The only snag was they played Nik Kershaw. He's ace but I hope he doesn't knock Frankie off the top spot. Frankie were ace of course. Holly was sweating like mad. OOOOH! Mum and Dad are real pains. Mum had the nerve to ask who was treading on Holly's foot when he went 'ow ow ow' at the start of Two Tribes. At least they agree that Tina Turner is an old bag. Scritti Politti were on too. Green's hair needed washing.

10th July
The video disco was ACE! The first video we saw was Two Tribes. We saw that twice, Relax once (it was the one with the tiger) and Girls on Film which wasn't all that bad, and Thriller. Thriller was terrible, especially when he turned into a zombie. I've waited yonks to see the Relax and Two Tribes videos. In Relax, Holly goes into this place (not a gay club) and gets on the wrong side of the people there, especially their fat leader (Nero) so he has a fight with the tiger. Joanne thought he was having it off with it! God he looked sexy. Then Nero pulled down his trousers! Two Tribes was

Reagan and Chernenko having a fight in a boxing ring. They grab each other in unmentionable places and stick their fingers up. Meanwhile, Holly and the boys watch.

6th August
HAD MY EARS PIERCED! They look really snazzy in little studs. I'm so happeeee, I found I could ignore a letter on Blue Suede Views saying that Relax and Two Tribes are awful, which on other days would have me snorting like a demented bull.

23rd August
The shops were extremely Wham! biased. They had about 1000 different Wham! keyrings, caps, T-shirts and pictures and only a very few crappy Duran ones. I expect the decent ones had sold out.

29th December
Blue Silver was FAB. Apart from the gig, it went right behind the scenes. At the end of one concert Simon and Andy were hugging each other, and they were all hysterical! Roger looked fab. I was crying when they were on stage. Can't wait till we go next year!

11th February, 1985
The BPI awards were mostly ace. Duran won Best Video with Wild Boys, Wham! Best Group (but D'ran weren't in that. Andrew looked really sexy!), Frankie Best Newcomers and Relax Best Single (of course, it's my all-time favourite!) and Paul Young Best Male Singer. Oh, and Prince won Best International Act. He looked a right wally – even had a bodyguard, and kept saying 'Thanks be to God'!

8th March
Interesting Fact: I am going off Wham! (although I still like Andy) already. I knew it wouldn't last because even Frankie paled out in

the end, although they monopolised last summer. I like George Michael sometimes, but not when he wins all the polls that Duran should win.

31st March
There was a Wham! interview in the Sunday paper. George said they wanted to be the biggest band in the world, and the bastards in the Express said, "They are, with the possible exception of Duran Duran, whom some critics believe are already on the wane". I had to scribble over that bit several times and draw moustaches on George Michael before I calmed down. That was the first time I thought, "I HATE WHAM!".

1st April
Hey, you'll never guess what? I saw Wham! on telly tonight and I was instantly converted! I am now a Wham! fan! I'll have to swap all my D'ran posters! ...HA HA HA!!!!!! APRIL FOOOOOOOOLLLLLL!! Bet I had you worried there! Take comfort, however, that even if it was essential (i.e. Duran split up), I would never go onto Wham! I'd go onto Paul Young, Nik, Howie, Frankie, Tears for Fears, etc. Never Wham! (sorry, Andrew).

9th May
We started on the 'Make a Duran Duran song using household implements' competition from Bruno Brookes. We're doing Girls on Film. Sandy is doing the camera bit with a whisk, Ros sings and I'm the drummer, using some spoons and telephone directories! Then, in the middle Sandy flushes the toilet, which sounds excellent.

Nobody can accuse us of not being original! We're taping the final version tomorrow and sending it to Bruno.

QUIZZING TIMES

Our school days may hold some great memories, but maths lessons are unlikely to be amongst them. However, this quiz will prove that MATHS CAN BE FUN! Simply use your knowledge of the 80s to fill in the missing numbers, and you'll soon be top of the class.

1 Members in Devo **X** Cylinder capacity for Stewart, Gouldman, Godley & Creme? **=** ?

2 Number of Swords for Tenpole Tudor's men **/** Loco In Acapulco Tops **=** ?

3 De La Soul's magic number **X** Pretenders' miles **=** ?

4 Starsound's stars **/** Breakfast Club members **=** ?

5 Number with the Ragged Tiger **X** Duran Duran UK No. 1 singles **=** ?

6 Paul Hardcastle's No. 1 single **+** Mike Lindup & Co's level **=** ?

7 Weeks at the top spot for Glenn Medeiros **-** Singles from FGTH's Pleasuredome album **=** ?

8 Status Quo's Gold Bars **+** Buck Rogers' centuries **=** ?

9 Saturday morning TV door number **-** Associates' Party Fears **=** ?

10 Members in Toto Coelo **+** Pirate Laser **=** ?

Up Close and Personal with Brother Beyond's Nathan Moore

Having spent 1987 and the first half of 1988 on the peripheries of the Top 40, Brother Beyond finally found success with the release of the Stock, Aitken & Waterman produced single 'The Harder I Try'. The band's success continued with their subsequent offerings 'He Ain't No Competition' and 'Be My Twin'. When Brother Beyond disbanded in 1991, lead singer Nathan Moore went on to front boy band Worlds Apart, whose following in France remains strong. A firm favourite on the 80's live music circuit, Nathan took time out ahead of his performance at a 48 Hour Party Weekend on the South Coast to chat about fame, family and fashion mistakes.

How did it then feel to be propelled into the spotlight with the No. 2 hit 'The Harder I Try'?

"In those days, if you went on and did Top of The Pops, the impact was so strong. When I think back, I can recall that moment walking down Oxford Street, the day after Top of The Pops aired, and nearly everybody was recognising me … I remember thinking 'I feel famous. This is bizarre.'"

How did you handle your newly found fame?

"The 'Yondies' found out where I lived in Islington, and there'd be this group of girls outside. I don't know why, but I climbed out the back window and along a wall. You know, why not just go out and talk to them? That's what the Bros boys did, didn't they? They just went out and talked to them, and their mum made tea and cakes. I should've used that approach."

Your mum may not have brought refreshments to your fans, but I've heard that they are likely to see her at your gigs.

"Mum nearly came to this one. She's good fun, my mum. She knows how to enjoy herself at … 75, I think she is now."

Does Nico (Nathan's 6 year old son) ever come to some of your family-friendly performances?

"He doesn't really like Daddy singing. He puts his ear defenders on!"

Fact: Nathan's middle name is Marcellus. The singer's father was hugely inspired by Muhammad Ali, born Cassius Marcellus Clay, and gave Nathan the same middle name in honour of the late boxing legend. Keeping with tradition, Nathan named his son Nico Marcellus Moore.

How real was the rivalry between Brother Beyond and Bros?

"The only rivalry we really had was Bros. I have met Matt [Goss] since. I said some unflattering things about him in Smash Hits. It was the biscuit tin or something in Smash Hits … and that was not the place to do it. Boy, those Brosettes!" [Nathan laughs] "Dangerous, lethal! They attacked my car once … spitting at it, banging on the windows, shouting obscenities."

What had you said to provoke such a response?

"I said something about his chest. I think he had some condition as a kid, and I made some joke … bad, I know … he was very sensitive to it. I've seen him a couple of times since, and we've done some charity things. He was fine, he's great. Today, it would have been a Twitter spat!"

Why do you think the Eighties continues to be so popular today?

"There were just some great bands, some great songs, and because it was about the song and because you had to have a strong image, it's really easy to remember the bands."

And to dress like them during 80's music weekends?

"Because there were such strong images, you can copy them, so they're perfect. That's how you dress to be Boy George, that's how you dress to be Adam Ant … there's an outfit for every band. My wife came to the last one, and went 'I'm going as Madonna'. Strong songs, strong image, and it's indelibly imprinted in our minds, isn't it?"

What was your worst fashion mistake of the Eighties?

"There was a few, wasn't there? We had these steel toe-capped DMs but we cut the toes out of them.

Carl Fysh [Brother Beyond's keyboards player] was always into his image … so I'd go along with certain things, then afterwards I'd think 'that looks horrendous. Why are we wearing that?' but you get railroaded into these things by this group mentality. They were always trying to put me in stuff to create the image: "Right, Nathan we want you to wear these braces.""

Thankfully, the braces are long gone, as are any other crimes against fashion he may have worn three decades ago. Saying goodbye to an ever-youthful Nathan Moore, it is hard to believe so much time has passed since then.

For an in depth interview with Nathan Moore look out for 'More Eighties', to be published in 2017.

Nathan Moore in action

1981

That was the year...

The Yorkshire Ripper was arrested

On 2nd January, following the discovery of false number plates on his vehicle, Peter Sutcliffe was detained by police. Further investigation of the area near Sutcliffe's Rover led to the discovery of a hammer and knife he had earlier discarded, giving the police the evidence they needed to charge the former gravedigger.

****

Ronald Reagan became 40th President of U.S.A.

The former Hollywood actor became the oldest President of the United States, when he defeated Jimmy Carter in the presidential campaign on 20th January. Later in the year, on 30th March, an unsuccessful assassination attempt was made on the new president's life when Reagan was shot by John Hinckley.

****

First London Marathon

Held on 29th March, the race saw 6,255 runners cross the finish line on Constitution Hill. American Dick Beardsley and Inge Simonsen of Norway held hands as they took joint first place in the men's race, with a time of 2:11:48. The women's race was won by British runner Joyce Smith, with a time of 2:29:57.

****

The SDP was formed

David Owen, Shirley Williams, Bill Rodgers and Roy Jenkins a.k.a. the Gang of Four launched their new political party on 26th March. The former Labour Party members established the Social Democratic Party as a middle ground between what they believed to be the increasing militant tendencies of the Labour Party and Thatcherism.

****

United Kingdom won Eurovision

Dublin played host to the 26th Eurovision Song Contest, which was held at the RDS Simmonscourt Pavilion, on 4th April. Beating the West German entry, Lena Valaitis, by four points, Bucks Fizz's performance of "Making Your Mind Up" secured the win for the UK. The song went on to spend 3 weeks at the top of the UK charts.

****

Pope John Paul II assassination attempt

Whilst riding through the Vatican in his 'Popemobile', on the morning of 13th May, the Pontiff was shot four times by Mehmet Ali Ağca. Sentenced to life imprisonment, Ağca was pardoned in 2000, following a request by the Pope, and deported to his native Turkey.

****

The Queen was under fire

During the Trooping The Colour ceremony on 13th June, Marcus Sarjeant fired six (blank) shots at Queen Elizabeth II as she rode along The Mall. Prosecuted under the Treason Act, he was sentenced to five years imprisonment.

****

Prince Charles married Lady Diana Spencer

The eyes of the world were upon London's St. Paul's Cathedral on 29th July, when the Prince of Wales married the 20 year old former nursery assistant. Diana's ivory silk taffeta wedding dress, designed by David and Elizabeth Emmanuel, featured a 25ft train

and was decorated with 10,000 pearls.

****

MTV aired in U.S.A.

Launched on 1st August, MTV fittingly featured "Video Killed The Radio Star" by The Buggles as the first video to be played by the channel.

****

Anarchy in the UK

Against a backdrop of increasing unemployment in recession-hit Britain, growing unrest and racial tension, a string of riots ran throughout the UK. London saw both the outbreak and conclusion of the unrest. Beginning in Brixton on 10th April and culminating with Handsworth's second riot, which ended on 11th September, the six month period also saw turmoil in areas of Liverpool (Toxteth), Leeds (Chapeltown), and Manchester (Moss Side).

****

Columbia returned to space

Having launched earlier in the year on 12th April, the space shuttle embarked on its second mission seven months later on 12th November, becoming the first manned spacecraft to be launched twice into space. It would go on to complete 25 further missions, before disintegrating upon re-entry in February 2003, killing all seven crew members.

****

We said a final goodbye to:

Bernard Lee, Bob Marley, Bill Haley, Bill Shankly, and Natalie Wood.

****

UK Chart Toppers included:

John Lennon
- Imagine & Woman

Soft Cell
- Tainted Love

Adam & The Ants
- Stand And Deliver & Prince Charming

Shakin' Stevens
- This Ole House & Green Door

Smokey Robinson
- Being With You

Dave Stewart & Barbara Gaskin
- It's My Party.

Top Films included:

Raiders of The Lost Ark, Chariots of Fire, Arthur, The Cannonball Run, and For Your Eyes Only.

****

Rear of The Year:

Felicity Kendal

FAIRGROUND

Clare and Debbie are looking forward to a day at the fair.

What ride shall we go on first?

How about the rollercoaster?

Maybe this wasn't such a great idea, we've been queuing for ages.

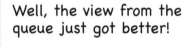

Well, the view from the queue just got better!

Try and look cool. Those girls are watching.

You've got to admit, he's gorgeous.

Well, I do like his yellow shirt.

Not him, the other one!

Looks like it's one each then!

Let me tell your fortune.

What does Zoltar predict?

It says "true love is a puzzle that rolls on by."

The Roller Disco!

I'm sorry. I really thought we would find him here.

There he is! But why is he playing with a Rubik's cube while he's skating?

Zoltar said "True love is a puzzle that rolls on by." He's my true love!

THE END

20 Questions
with Then Jerico's
Mark Shaw

First hitting the UK Top 20 in 1987 with 'The Motive (Living Without You)', Then Jerico went on to enjoy chart success throughout the latter part of the decade with tracks such as 'Big Area' and 'Sugar Box'.

The band's split in 1990 led to the release the following year of lead singer Mark Shaw's solo album, 'Almost', produced by Duran Duran's Andy Taylor.

Still performing Then Jerico's material on the 80's retro circuit, Mark Shaw took time out to ponder some probing questions.

****

1. What is your favourite 80's song?
Teenage Wildlife by David Bowie.

****

2. What was the best 80's TV programme?
The Tube.

****

3. Who was your teenage crush?
Lesley-Anne Down / Debbie Harry.

****

4. What was your favourite subject at school?
Music!

****

5. What job would you have done if you hadn't been a singer?
Record Producer.

****

6. What was your worst fashion mistake of the 80s?
Getting my hair extensions cut off at the sides into an accidental semi-mullet.

****

7. What was your first car?
Rover P5.

****

8. What was the first single you ever bought?
Reach Out (I'll Be There) by The Four Tops.

****

9. Where did you perform your first gig?
Monkberry's nightclub, London.

****

10. Where is the best place you have ever visited?
Pompeii.

****

11. Which five people, living or dead, would be your ideal dinner guests?

David Bowie, Mozart, Attila the Hun, Anaïs Nin and Laura Shaw (my wife).

****

12. Which pet hate would you consign to Room 101?
Canned laughter.

****

13. What makes you angry?
Hypocrisy.

****

14. What was the last film you watched?
Coffee Town.

****

15. What are you most proud of?
Headlining gig at The Albert Hall.

****

16. What would be your perfect day?
Listening to music and relaxing with my lady in a private water villa in the Indian Ocean.

****

17. What is the best Christmas present you've ever had?
A beautiful Prada bag (from Laura).

****

18. And the worst?
A pair of pink Duran Duran slippers.

****

19. What do you want for Christmas this year?
A new hat.

****

20. What are your hopes for the future?
An end to the pointless violence of terrorism, and new laws to protect animals against cruelty.

****

Then Jerico
in action

Jimmy Helms *holding his copy of "Your Eighties"*

In The Comfort Zone with Jimmy Helms

First enjoying UK chart success in 1973, with the No. 2 hit 'Gonna Make You An Offer You Can't Refuse', Jimmy Helms returned to the Top 20 at the end of 1988 when, as part of Londonbeat, he brought us the gorgeous harmonies of '9 A.M. (The Comfort Zone)'. Best known for their 1990 single 'I've Been Thinking About You', Londonbeat disbanded in 1995, only to regroup in 2003. The current line-up comprises of Jimmy Helms, Jimmy Chambers (both were backing vocalists on Paul Young's 1985 album 'The Secret of Association') and Myles Kayne.

A veteran performer, Jimmy talks about music through the decades and the changes he has seen.

****

How does the music industry now compare to when you first started out?

"It's different in the way that I think. When I was starting out, record companies were a way of getting yourself heard on the radio, seen on television. That was your promotion plan. Now, the record companies have gone, and it is down to performers who are able to sing live. They're the ones who survive [not] the ones who were kinda tap dancing on stage and not really singing, not really putting it out … the studio production kind of singers … the Milli Vanilli sort of singing. I think now what you see on stage is people who are actually able to stand in front of an audience and sing a song."

****

What was the first record you ever bought?

"The first record I bought was probably James Brown and The Famous Flames, a song called … [Jimmy bursts into song] "Please, please, please, please" … that one. That and Little Richard's first records, that era of music, that's what I'm talking about. But there was a point before then, when I was listening to radio, and I was hearing the music that became R&B. There was a lady who sang and played guitar, Sister Rosetta [Tharpe]. She's very important … the mother of R&B music."

****

So, what was your favourite decade for music?

"My favourite decade for music would have to be … Can I be greedy and have two? There's the era of Jazz … Miles Davis, even what he did later on. The acoustic era of Jazz, I'm talking about that … late Fifties, Sixties. Then later on, because I'm a fan of all kinds of music … Tamla Motown, The Beatles … all of it came together at the time of Woodstock. That kinda sums it up for me because you've got all these things together … Miles Davis, Jimi Hendrix … all these different music forms."

****

Why do you think today's retro festivals have become so popular?

"It's a lot of that same energy, the same love of being outside. I think being outside has a certain something. It's energising in a way that music's not when it's inside."

****

Who were your musical influences?

"For singing, I go back to Johnny Mathis, Sam Cooke, Jackie Wilson. There's a cross of a lot of different styles, and learning to appreciate different styles of music. Frank Sinatra, Marvin Gaye … it goes on and on and on. Tell me when to stop!" [Jimmy laughs].

****

Have you got a favourite track you like to perform?

"My favourite track to perform has got to be the Londonbeat song, 9 A.M." [I tell Jimmy it's my favourite Londonbeat track, and show him my notes where I've written words to that effect]. "We're going to do an acapella version right at the start of the show … you can look forward to that."

Look forward to it I did, and I was not disappointed as the Londonbeat trio delighted us with a gloriously soulful and upbeat set.

1982 That was the year...

Mark Thatcher disappeared

The Prime Minister's son, his co-driver and mechanic went missing for six days in the Sahara Desert, whilst competing in the Dakar Rally. Having strayed over 30 miles off course, the group were eventually discovered by Algerian military on 14th January.

****

The Falklands War

Argentina's invasion of the Falkland Islands on the 2nd April led to a British task force being sent to reclaim the islands. Following fierce fighting and a British victory in the Battle of Goose Green, Argentina surrendered on 14th June. During the conflict, 255 British and 655 Argentine servicemen, along with three Falkland Islanders, lost their lives.

****

Fame fever hit the UK

Scheduled to air immediately after Top of The Pops, the first episode of Fame was broadcast in the UK on 17th June. The series quickly gained huge popularity, producing Top 40 singles "Fame", "Starmaker" and "Hi-Fidelity", not to mention a nation of leg-warmer wearing teenagers!

****

Buckingham Palace had an intruder

Michael Fagan, an unemployed decorator, managed to breach Royal security and break into the Queen's bedroom on 9th July. The 33 year old spent ten minutes in her Majesty's presence, before being removed by palace police.

****

The first CD player went on sale

Manufactured by Sony, the CDP-101 was released in Japan on 1st October. However, it would be another six months before the system was launched worldwide.

****

The Mary Rose resurfaced

Having sunk in 1545, during the Battle of The Solent, the flagship of Henry VIII's fleet was salvaged on 16th October. Thanks to regular reports from children's TV show Blue Peter, thousands of kids tuned in to watch as the wreck was finally lifted from the sea bed.

****

Channel 4 was launched

Broadcasting began at 4.45pm on 2nd November, with the voice of Paul Coia welcoming everyone to the channel, before the airing of its first programme "Countdown".

****

The Tube was first broadcast

Presented by Paula Yates and Jools Holland, the Channel 4 music show first aired on 5th November. Punk band The Toy Dolls (of Nellie The Elephant fame) were the first band to play on the programme.

****

Michael Jackson's Thriller was released

The best-selling album of all time, Thriller entered the UK charts at Number 29 on 11th December. It stayed in the charts for 131 consecutive weeks, until June 1985, and has returned numerous times since.

****

A human chain was formed around Greenham Common

Encompassing the 9 mile perimeter fence at the RAF military base, 30,000 women held hands on 12th December, in protest against the decision to site American cruise missiles there.

****

We said a final goodbye to:

Arthur Lowe, Grace Kelly, Harry H. Corbett, Ingrid

Bergman, John Belushi and Marty Feldman.

****

UK Chart Toppers included:

Bucks Fizz
- Land of Make Believe & My Camera Never Lies

The Goombay Dance Band
- Seven Tears

Dexys Midnight Runners - Come On Eileen

Madness
- House of Fun

The Jam
- A Town Called Malice/Precious & Beat Surrender

Musical Youth
- Pass The Dutchie

Culture Club
- Do You Really Want To Hurt Me?

****

Top Films included:

E.T., The Snowman, Gandhi, Blade Runner, Tootsie, Conan The Barbarian, Tron, Annie, An Officer and A Gentleman, 48 Hrs, Star Trek II: The Wrath of Khan.

****

Rear of The Year:

Suzi Quatro

LYRICALLY CHALLENGED

Anyone who has ever sung "I'm a prima donna" to UB40's Food For Thought knows how challenging it can be to identify the correct lyrics of a song. How many of these lines from UK Top 40 singles do you recognise?

1. I'm hiding from you and your soul of ice.

2. I had a dream there was a rainbow, over the mountains, over the sea.

3. A man so large he barely fit his circumstances.

4. Tore down the House of Commons in your brand new shoes.

5. Respect yourself and all of those around you.

6. It's a Daisy age and you're about to walk top stage.

7. And Catch 22 says if I sing the truth, they won't make me an overnight star.

8. These mist-covered mountains are a home for me now.

9. Riding through dust clouds and barren wastes, galloping hard on the plains.

10. I read all the newspapers but my mother still reads my mail.

11. Trying hard to control my heart, I walk over to where you are.

12. There's nothing I wouldn't do, including doing nothing.

13. All the pathos you can keep for the children in the street.

14. Is it the pain of the drinking or the Sunday sinking feeling?

15. Waiting with his neighbours in the rush hour queue.

16. He let me know a secret about the money in his kitty.

17. Academic inspiration, you gave me none.

18. You were the one that they'd talk about around town, as they put you down.

19. Just like the old man in that book by Nabokov.

20. I said so many things, things he didn't know.

21. Something nasty in your garden's waiting patiently 'til it can have your heart.

22. There's a fine line drawing my senses together, and I think it's about to break.

23. You got the kinda legs that do more than walk.

24. She had the nerve to ask me if I planned to do her any harm.

25. Feel like a child on a dark night, wishing there was some kind of heaven.

Answers at back of book

26

80's FASHION WORDSEARCH

```
V T U F J T R P Y V S J C P M N B S P W
S M R U I I A B W H Z O R I K B A T E L
S V B I A N K R E B R Z N X D T T N M O
C Z U H H F G L T K W E X I S S W A S U
X I G T X S L E S A D H M E S N I P R M
T I U H S S T C R E N H L B M O N I B S
B R H C U I R N L L C F F O A O G K I E
R H N I A E A B A I E L Y O E D S S Y L
X C T J W L U W K G L S Y T Z O L E H L
J S D P O O E G H N O Z S S M I E V Q I
W G E G D E E G T G O L B G O V E X M R
Y R M U L L E T W Z I U S X L M V Z A D
M V T R I K S A R A R H J S Z O E T Q A
I I K L O W M P L L R C B I J B V C Q P
C Y L T W V P E X U T M W S D P Z E R S
O O N W S H Y B Z H Y E E I Z R W X S E
S D A P R E D L U O H S U R D E E Q U U
F R I L L Y S H I R T Y T L S G I J M R
Y G B L K X A G I J M Q Z D G K V K A L
Z O C V W S I H K W D N B X Y G P I W F
```

Batwing sleeve	**Frilly shirt**	**Shell suits**
Big hair	**High waist**	**Shoulder pads**
Corkscrew perm	**Legwarmers**	**Ski pants**
Double denim	**Mullet**	**Slogan T-shirt**
Espadrilles	**Pixie boots**	**Snood**
Fingerless gloves	**Ra-ra skirt**	**Tartan**

Answers at back of book

STYLE COUNSELLING

Many of the outfits we donned in the Eighties were memorable, although there are a few that are best forgotten. I asked some of our favourite 80's artists to reveal the worst fashion mistakes they made during the decade that good taste forgot.

"My biggest fashion faux pas was allowing the film set hairdresser to back-comb my hair for my close up in the St Elmo's video. I used to have my hair permed back then, and if you back-comb a perm the hair just explodes. Hence my bobbing pompadour as I am singing the song. I knew it was bad then, even when everything in the 80s was larger than life!"
John Parr

"All of it!"
Nick Beggs, Kajagoogoo

"I dyed my pubic hair pink."
Clive Jackson, Dr & The Medics

"My look for the 'I Hear Talk' video. My hair too ... a big disaster as I had extensions in, due to a perm solution being left on for nearly an hour. It fell out in clumps. The extensions were nylon so they melted when curled on set. A domino effect! The pink leather coat covered up the fact I had put on 6lb in weight. In my book then, shameful."
Jay Aston, Bucks Fizz

"I don't know if it's Seventies ... yeah, I'm thinking of the late Seventies ... kipper ties and ginormous lapels, but that was more like The Sweeney period, wasn't it? The Eighties ... I don't know. Were Oxford Bags in the Eighties? Probably those. You could get two legs in one trouser!"
Bruce Foxton

"As a guy, the Eighties were brilliant because you could wear a designer suit, very cutting edge fashion. You could wear eyeliner and still be quite masculine. I think men's fashion has become very bland by comparison. I think Johnny Hates Jazz were one of the better dressed bands. We didn't wear anything that was embarrassing. One of my brothers worked at a fashion store in the King's Road, and they supplied us with all our clothes just before they got released to the public."
Clark Datchler, Johnny Hates Jazz.

"Leather jeans."
Dave Brewis, The Kane Gang

"Black ballet pumps and yellow trousers ... a multitude of fashion faux pas."
Owen Paul

"Wow, many I guess. I had a pair of silver boots made by Nike that I bought in Rome, and I had a good few Peronis beforehand … made them look better than they actually were. Think I still have them in the garage!"
Paul Hardcastle

"I was a real Soul Boy. I wore jazz shoes all the time, everywhere. That wasn't as bad as the legwarmers. You think, at the time, it's trendy."
Andy Kyriacou, Modern Romance

"Big hair! Shoulder pads! There were lots. I wanted an outfit like Diana Ross wore in her video for "Pieces of Ice". She had this tip to toe sequined bodysuit on. I had one made, because I could. I wore it a few times, but never on TV."
Hazell Dean

"It was the diver's suit. I thought 'What a great idea…' until I realised how heavy it was."
Buster Bloodvessel

"There's so many, so many … too many to mention. The thing is, I unashamedly loved the flamboyancy!"
Phil Fearon

"I did do a TV show in a crop top which, on reflection, was maybe a wee bit out there."
Ian Donaldson, H2O

"I had some nice leather pants."
Dennis Seaton, Musical Youth

"A giant rosary bought in Ibiza in 1989 worn round the neck. The beads were the size of ping pong balls."
Richard Coles, The Communards

"If it's comfortable, I'm happy. I hate being hot in clothes. My shoes always tend to be flip-flops or flip-flops with socks!"
Jona Lewie

"I steered well clear of any mainstream fashion. I mostly made all of my clothes myself and rarely bought anything from a shop. I can honestly say that I still love all the things I wore throughout the 80s, and I never cringe when I see photos of me from that time. Boring, I know, but true!"
Jill Bryson, Strawberry Switchblade

"There were no crimes against taste in pop, but I came pretty close."
Martin Fry

Phil Fearon can still Prove It

A quartet of Top 10 hits with Galaxy, including 'Everybody's Laughing' and 'Dancing Tight', firmly secured Phil Fearon's place in the memories of 80's music fans.

Following the release of 'Ain't Nothing But A Houseparty' at the end of 1986, the singer took a break from the limelight to set up his own record label, Production House Records. The label included 90's rave acts such as Baby D, whose No. 1 single 'Let Me Be Your Fantasy' featured Phil's wife Dee Galdes on lead vocals.

The former Galaxy front man returned to the stage in 2010, and continues to perform on the retro circuit. Here, he talks about his memories of the Eighties and the changing face of popular music.

****

Why do you think Eighties' music has remained so popular?

"I'm not sure. My kids love the Eighties. I hear records playing and I think they won't know this, but they know all the lyrics. So, I'm not sure. I think maybe it's an overhang of the Seventies with Club music, when going out and getting dressed up became the 'in' thing. I'm just glad it is."

****

How does performing now compare with the Eighties?

"It's just as much fun as then. I've always loved it. I think now, you just feel more grateful." [Phil laughs].

****

Does it feel like there is less pressure now?

"It feels like there's less pressure because you've done it for quite a while now, and you've nothing to prove. Often at 80's gigs, the audience is already on your side so there's no pressure that way. It's like a reunion."

****

Is there anything you miss about the Eighties?

"It was exciting. There's nothing better than putting a record out and waiting to see where it charts the next week. Sitting there, waiting for the 'phone call … all that excitement in that whole era, I do miss that."

****

What was the first single you ever bought?

"I remember the first single us kids bought … me, my brother and sister. It was The Monkees' Daydream Believer."

****

Who are your musical influences?

"Oh, my goodness … everything! It's all down to the record. My influences are genuinely varied. When I was growing up, my dad used to play a lot of Country & Western, and I love that stuff. Being Jamaican born, reggae … that's my upbringing. You come to my house and one day you'll hear me play Bob Marley, another day it'll be Julio Iglesias. Whenever I'm doing paperwork, it's always classical music I play. The only thing I never quite got into was Punk, even though I was almost a member of the Sex Pistols."

****

Really? So, what happened?

"I got offered to join them. I went to school with the bass player, Glen Matlock. He's a friend of mine. He came round and said they're putting this band together, they haven't got a keyboard player, come down to Chelsea and meet the band. I was 'uh, I'll let you know'."

****

What are your thoughts on how the music industry has changed since the Eighties?

"There's something that happened when recorded music started coming out regularly … to the memories. In the old days, if you heard something and loved it, you may not hear it again for a while.

Now, everything's recorded and things have gone too far. There's so much access, there's so much music, you kinda get lost in it. I think the current generation get so much stuff they're flooded with it, but back then it was appreciated.

You bought the record, you bought the posters, and it was something special. They get so much for free, I don't think it's got the same kind of kudos. [In] the Sixties, Seventies, Eighties the music felt like it's got special value."

SECRET 80's DIARY

The Untrendy Teenager's Thoughts on...

Posters, Roger Taylor and The Young Ones

11th April, 1984

I'm thinking of putting my Limahl posters on the ceiling so all the walls can be for Duran. Frankie posters have the door and Fraggles posters the wardrobe.

16th April

I love Roger Taylor more than ever. I go all gaga when I think of him. I LUV ROGER - IDST [If destroyed, still true].

22nd April

The Young Ones was ACE! You'll never guess what Rik did. Well, he was trying to impress a girl and found a tampon in her bag. Unsuspecting, he started going "Ooh, a present for me. Can you smoke it? It's like a little mouse! Mousy, mousy!" Honestly, I think that was the funniest bit ever. Even Mum was smiling. I was nearly dying with laughter! How Rik can do that without laughing beats me. Can't wait till next week. RIK, I LOVE YOU!

5th May

Bought The Reflex and Roger poster. It's gorgeous. Sleeve of

The Reflex is a giant poster. Bought 'I Love You' sticker from The Treasure Trove and stuck it on Roger. Looked up 'Roger' in first names dictionary. It means 'fame spear'. Got more Smash Hits stickers, including Marilyn and loads of swaps. Got Mark White from ABC again!

8th May

Watched The Young Ones. It is FAB, even better than the Fraggles! Vyvyan was kicking his head about and they killed his sock. My favourite is Vyvyan (isn't that a girl's name?) but I can't stand Neil the hippy. Alexei Sayle was in it too. Can't wait till next week. Mum called Vyvyan a 'revolting specimen'. I think he's really great. Not as nice as Roger though!

11th May

This morning found me in a really bad mood, on being told that as we were having our chimney done up, all the TV aerials had to come out, which meant I couldn't see The Young Ones. I just broke down and cried. Getting no

sympathy whatsoever.

12th May

Swapped around Duran posters. The Roger one is now nearly over my bed. I was given this ace poster yesterday. It's got Roger and Andy on it. Got Smash Hits. There was a feature about Boy George, Tina Turner etc. Boy George said Frankie were stupid. Grrrr! I like Marilyn better than him now.

29th May

The Young Ones was great. Vyvyan and Rik were ace, as usual. Mum wasn't pleased cos they were shouting out 'bastard', but I don't think Gran heard.

30th May

Princess Margaret has called Boy George a 'made up tart'. Well said, old chappess!

5th June

The Young Ones was FAB. Rik's still a virgin – he wouldn't be if I had any say in the matter. Yeah, he's sweet! Of course, I still love Roger best. Oooh I could ******* him to death! What, Mike Read? You're banning this entry? You're the pits, man!

21st June
Got Smash Hits. Discovered that Roger's gonna get married (pause to tear out hair). Oh Roger, why do you have to do this to me? At least Holly can never get married.

26th June
Roger, you lovesick little rat! You're supposed to marry ME! No, not really, love. I forgive ya. After all, Rik is perhaps still available.

1st July
I am very depressed tonight. The Young Ones has finished, and don't blame me if there's a teardrop on the page. It's been on so long that it hasn't hit me that it's finished. I'm sure I'll die. I can't live without gorgeous Rik. Rik (sniff) I want you to know that nothing will ever replace The Young Ones. I still love you and I always will. You've made me laugh, cry, crazy and The Young Ones will always be one of the most lovable things I'll look back on. It's been an important time in my life and nothing will ever be the same. Thanks, Rik for the Young Ones, the hours of pleasure, for being so lovely, and for being YOU!

24th November
I'm now faced with more Frankie posters than space or Blu Tack can handle and, after an agonising think, I've decided to take down the big Smash Hits one that used a lot of Blu Tack, and a Holly one that's a double.

13th January, 1985
Rearranged my posters for the first time in yonks. Took down the Nik Kershaw and Howard Jones ones, just kept the two big ones from Smash Hits on the door. Put Limahl on the wardrobe, except

the big one which went where Howard used to be. Most of the Frankie ones managed to fit into Limahl's old corner. Now there's lots of space for Duran.

18th January
Several people brought me Duran posters today – at least 10. I like this swapping. Smash Hits is good - there's a Simon le Bon poster and a Nik Kershaw one, and facts about Frankie. There is a bitchy letter that made me SEETHE. Some moron wrote in asking why Roger's wedding beat the Miners' Strike in the Smash Hits Poll Most Important Event of 1984. Had the nerve to call it 'trivial'! Poor Roger, it wasn't trivial to him. If that sod had thought about the heartbreak/happiness I'd felt, too. Ignore him, Roger baby.

2nd February
I bought a really big Duran poster mag for only £1. It was a Valentine special, but the only snag was it had Simon and John on the main bit and the other three on half of the back. They should have all been on the front really, but it's still ace! So, changed some posters round when I got home. Result: I now have one Frankie poster (the

one that came free with the 12" of Two Tribes) on my wardrobe with a Limahl one. Duran are all over the place. I would love one of the duvet and pillow case sets from the magazine, with a big heart saying one of their names in the middle. I'd go for Roger, of course.

6th March
Debbie has heard somewhere that Duran are splitting up. I shouldn't think it's true, people are always saying it. She had a Jackie with a pic of Duran. Roger and John were topless. John looked a wimp (sorry JT) but Roger's body is – WOWWWW! He was only wearing a pair of little shorts! Everyone was going mad, especially me!

3rd November
Went round Claire's at about 6pm wearing my Duran scarf, badges, cap, sweatbands, Roger earrings and carrying my Duran briefcase. Claire and I wrote some more of our stories, pretending we were with Simon and Roger. Inspired by her, I wrote things like "Our mouths melted together and we snogged for 5 minutes. I had wanted him ever since I was 13, and now it was true!"

1983 That was the year...

Breakfast TV launched

BBC's Breakfast Time, the UK's first breakfast TV show, made its debut broadcast on 17th January. ITV were soon to follow the Beeb's lead, with the launch of TV-am on 1st February.

****

The UK belted up

The wearing of seatbelts by drivers and front passengers became compulsory on 31st January. It was another six years before rear seatbelts were required to be worn by under-14s, and two more years for that law to be extended to all passengers.

****

Motown celebrated its 25th Anniversary

The Motown 25 celebrations were held at the Pasadena Civic Auditorium, California on 25th March. Amongst those taking to the stage that evening was Michael Jackson. During his performance of Billie Jean, he showed off his Moonwalk, learnt from Shalamar's Jeffrey Daniel.

****

The Pound was coined

The pound coin was introduced as currency in England and Wales on 21st April. Chancellor Nigel Lawson announced, on 12th November 1984, that the pound note was to be replaced by the new coin. One pound notes were finally withdrawn from circulation in the UK on 11th March 1988.

****

Hitler's Diaries were discovered

There was a media frenzy as newspapers fought for exclusive rights to the Führer's journals, following German magazine Stern's announcement of their existence, on 22nd April. Within a fortnight, the diaries were forensically proven to be fake, the work of serial forger Konrad Kujau.

****

Margaret Thatcher was re-elected

Following a landslide victory in the 9th June General Election, the Conservative government remained in power in the UK. With a majority of 144 seats, it was the most decisive election victory since that of Labour in 1945.

****

Blockbusters arrived

The afternoon gameshow, hosted by Bob Holness, was first broadcast on 29th August. The show featured sixth formers as contestants, who soon became eager to ask their host "Can I have a P please, Bob?"!

****

Vanessa Williams made American history

The actress and singer was crowned Miss America on 17th September, having entered the competition as Miss New York. She became the first black woman to win the title. However, her reign was brought to a premature end, following the publication by Penthouse of nude photos of the former model. On 23rd July 1984, the 21-year-old resigned from her role, the first resignation in the pageant's history.

****

Neil Kinnock replaced Michael Foot

The Labour Party's heavy election defeat earlier in the year had resulted in Michael Foot's resignation just three days later. A leadership contest followed, in which Kinnock gained 71% of the vote, becoming Labour's new leader on 2nd October.

****

Walton Sextuplets born

Following fertility treatment, Jane Walton gave birth to six baby girls on 18th November, in Liverpool. They became the world's first all-female sextuplets to survive.

****

Brink's-Mat Heist

Led by Brian Robinson and Micky McAvoy, a gang of six broke in to the vault at Heathrow Airport on 26th November. They stole gold bullion worth almost £26 million. The only gang members to be convicted of the crime, Robinson and McAvoy each received a 25 year jail sentence for their roles in the robbery. However, there have been over 20 untimely deaths related to those involved since the heist took place.

****

We said a final goodbye to:

Billy Fury, David Niven, Dick Emery, John Le Mesurier, Karen Carpenter, Tennessee Williams and Violet Carson.

****

UK Chart Toppers included:

Culture Club
- Karma Chameleon
Spandau Ballet
- True

Kajagoogoo
- Too Shy
Billy Joel
- Uptown Girl
Paul Young
- Wherever I Lay My Hat
David Bowie
- Let's Dance
The Police
- Every Breath You Take.

****

Top Films included:

Flashdance, Risky Business, Trading Places, Octopussy, Krull, Merry Christmas Mr. Lawrence, Educating Rita, The Outsiders, Return of The Jedi, and Jaws 3-D.

****

Rear of The Year:

Lulu

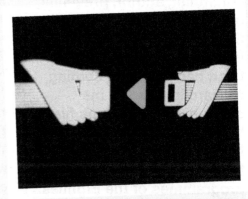

Garry Bushell's Top 10 of 80's TV

Music journalist, newspaper columnist, author, presenter, or frontman for Oi! band The Gonads. Whichever guise he is in, Garry Bushell has never been backwards in coming forward in offering his opinion. Here, he dons his "Bushell On The Box" cap, to tell us what he believes were the best television programmes of the Eighties.

****

Minder

Arthur Daley was a spiv with pretentions, ducking and diving his way through dodgy deals with only his minder, two-fisted Terry McCann to keep him safe. Brilliantly written and superbly acted, this Euston Films series was devised by Leon Griffiths and lovingly celebrated London's seedy underbelly. At its height, Minder attracted 16.4million viewers. Its colourful characters and phrases passed into folklore: "I'll have a large VAT Dave, on the slate of course".

****

Only Fools & Horses

Without question, the greatest British sitcom of the 80s (and 90s). Del Boy Trotter may have looked like a low rent Arthur Daley to start with, but viewers took him, and the rest of the characters John Sullivan created, to their hearts. Only Fools was an above average comedy that grew organically into a national institution, thanks to the warmth and heart of John's writing and the marvellous cast. We felt Del's pain and we shared his dreams. If you were like me, you were also gutted when he lost his fortune.

****

Dallas

The big daddy of soap operas, with one of TV's all time most captivating villains. Larry Hagman sparkled as cheating Texan oilman J.R. Ewing, the man we loved to hate. Such was his appeal that, when JR got shot in 1980, 83 million Americans and 24 million British viewers tuned in to see whodunnit. The storyline made such an impact, EastEnders has endlessly recycled it.

****

Star Trek – The Next Generation

I loved the original Star Trek so much, I was convinced Picard and Riker could never replace Kirk and Spock in my affections. I was wrong. The Next Generation was a tremendous addition to TV sci-fi, chock full of great ideas (The Borg, the Holodeck) and huge characters (like Q, Worf, Deanna Troy, and Data). It ran for seven seasons and very rarely disappointed.

****

Auf Wiedersehen, Pet

You wouldn't have thought the story of a mob of hairy-arsed English building workers, labouring in Düsseldorf, would touch the nation - but it did. Millions took these down to earth characters to their hearts. The show made Jimmy Nail a star, and featured the late great rock 'n' roller Gary Holton as Cockney Wayne.

****

Cheers

The Boston bar where everybody knew your name. One of many strong US sitcoms of the 1980s, made extra special by sharp writing and well-rounded characters; none more rounded than Norm Peterson. And, of course, Cheers spawned Frasier, which is still a joy to this day. Seinfeld began in 1989 but didn't reach stellar heights until the Nineties.

****

Boys From The Blackstuff

Alan Bleasdale's warm but often heart-wrenching story of working class Scousers struggling to get by in the unemployment-blitzed early 80s. Few who saw it will ever forget Bernard Hills as head-butting Yosser Hughes, and his catchphrase "Gizza job. I can do that."

****

Blackadder Goes Forth

The last and best of the four Blackadder series. Goes Forth was set in a Flanders trench during the Battle of the Somme, with our doomed heroes under the incompetent command of Stephen Fry's supremely pompous General Melchett. Poignant and thought-provoking, as well as funny.

****

Fox
A Euston Films drama series about working class loyalty, masculinity and occasional villainy. Set around a large South London family, Fox featured Peter Vaughan as the Dad, a former market porter whose sons included Bernard Hill and Ray Winstone, who played Kenny, a boxer. Someone should repeat it.

****

The Young Ones
The first, and arguably the best, TV to come from what was then called alternative comedy. The anarchic BBC 2 sitcom helped break Alexei Sayle, Rik Mayall and Ade Edmondson, and also featured musical guests including Madness and The Damned. The follow-up, Filthy Rich & Catflap bombed like Sir Arthur Harris.

****

Runners-up:
Out, Widows, Roseanne, Married With Children, Rumpole, Twin Peaks, The A-Team, Lovejoy, Moonlighting
... how long have you got??

Turning back the clock with Clark Datchler of Johnny Hates Jazz

The late Eighties saw Johnny Hates Jazz reach the height of their success with hit singles 'Shattered Dreams', 'I Don't Want To Be A Hero' and 'Turn Back The Clock'. Comprised of lead vocalist Clark Datchler, guitarist Mike Nocito, and Calvin Hayes on keyboards, the band's rise up the charts was arguably destined, given the heritage of some of the band members. Clark's father, Fred Datchler, was the saxophonist with the Stargazers, the first British band to top the UK Singles Chart, and Calvin the son of legendary producer and record label boss, Mickie Most.

At the end of 1988, Clark left the band to pursue a solo career. Johnny Hates Jazz subsequently broke up, only to be reformed in 2009 when the singer and Mike Nocito were reunited. Their highly acclaimed album 'Magnetized' was released in 2013, and the pair continue to record and tour. I caught up with Clark this summer, to talk about music, performing and changing face of the record industry.

****

Where was the first gig you played?

"The first Johnny Hates Jazz gig was at Ronnie Scott's. It was a showcase for record labels. We'd already had one single out on RAK Records, Mickie Most's label, Me And My Foolish Heart. It got good reviews but was not a hit, so we decided to change labels. We thought we would do a showcase at Ronnie Scott's as Johnny Hates Jazz. We thought it was very funny, of course, the premier jazz club featuring Johnny Hates Jazz. We invited people from the record labels, and I think three of the labels showed up. We played acoustically. As we did the set, one by one,

each of them left, except one person stayed. His name was John Wooler and he signed us to Virgin Records. That's when we first had our success. It was his ears that saved the day."

****

Did you perform live before Johnny Hates Jazz?

"I first started song writing when I was eight. You don't want to hear that stuff. It was terrible. Then, you naturally start

playing live in those school situations. remember I went on holiday with a fri of mine to Ibiza before it became the I that it is now. I did a performance in a … just impromptu. There were a coup performers there and I said 'Can I hav go?'. They begrudgingly let me … I wa only probably 15. I did a couple of so and I had a standing ovation.

The other performers threw me out aft that!"

That must give you a thirst for performing?

"It does, but you have to remember that we emerged from the 1980s, which was the era when playing live was secondary to recording. We lived in studios. That was where we wanted to be, the recording studio. Then you'd tour and play live as a consequence of that. Now, it's the other way round."

****

It does seem to be that the 80's acts who have remained popular on the live retro circuits are actually those who were most successful as recording artists.

"That's right, and we're all having to get used to the fact that this is the world that we live in, which is fine. It's just different."

****

You still did some live performances during the Eighties, so how do they compare with going on stage now?

"Well, Johnny Hates Jazz didn't do a lot of live stuff, to be honest. We'd each individually done a lot of live stuff before that, but you did live stuff really as a means to get a record deal. Record deals have no purpose any more. The major record labels have their place, but they don't have nearly the influence they used to have. Now, really you're playing live for the sake of playing live, as a way to bring your music to the audience as the first port of call."

****

That shift within the music industry must mean you have witnessed a lot of change.

"But, one thing that doesn't change is this is all about communication. It's very easy for people in music to get cynical and talk only about money. If you write a song or play an instrument and you perform live, you want to communicate. That's probably because when you were younger, you struggled with ways to express yourself in conventional society, so you found other ways. That's what all this is about, and if you can communicate with an audience, they want to communicate back with you. It's a wonderful thing."

****

Would you say that is the key to why retro festivals are so successful?

"I think it's a cultural shift. In the Eighties, people did go and see bands live, but you went out and you bought physical records, and CDs eventually. That became your most prized item. Now, your live ticket is your most prized item because no one owns any physical product unless you're a die-hard and you go and buy vinyl. I think also that people like to be outside. It's a way to get out of a world that's becoming increasingly within a built up environment … it's important to people to be in a natural environment."

****

The festivals seem to cover a wide demographic too.

"It's always amazing at these gigs, and I'll be doing this later, I ask them about the age groups. It's surprising how many young people come to these gigs, and they are often the ones who are first in line for autographs at the end. It's like we discovered when we grew up … we were children of the Sixties, Seventies … I certainly am. That's how the music of the Eighties came in to being. It was because of those previous decades, and these kids want to know where their music came from. Even though I'd say there's more of a disconnect now between current chart music and music of previous decades, they still want that sense of history."

****

Is there anything you miss about the Eighties?

"I'm not someone that harkens back to the past too much. You see, my dad was a professional jazz musician, very successful. He had great difficulty in accepting what happened to him in the Sixties, in the advent of rock 'n' roll in Britain, because The Beatles essentially put all the jazz musicians out of work. I understand now that jazz music operated in a different way. I understand that struggle with how the world is moving and how you find your place in that, but a lot of the jazz musicians didn't and that was it … [it was] very sad. We're fortunate in that we can keep on going in our own way. So, I predicate everything I say on that … In the Eighties, Seventies and Sixties, music was often in the chart which really had something to say. They had social, political messages, environmental messages. It was commonplace, it was just something you did. That stemmed from the beatniks in the Fifties, then the Sixties happened, the Peace Movement, etc. So, you think back on the Eighties, it was no different. It was very common for songs with something to say to be very high in the charts. I think that influenced society in its way. It can't do that now. I'm not saying people don't make music of consciousness, they do. Certainly, rap music seems to have held onto that mantle, but it's very specific to that world. As far as global observations, statements and concerns … you don't find that in chart music anymore. People still make it, but it won't be supported, and I miss that."

****

Would you say it has produced a generation struck by apathy?

"It's a generation that are addicted to entertainment. We never thought of ourselves as entertainment. As a musician in the Eighties, Seventies and Sixties, it was considered the lowest of the lowest things to go on a TV show and present, or be in an advertisement. Now … I remember listening to the Top 40 last week. One song came on and they immediately said "this record was in the Fiat 500 commercial, it's doing really well". That's a turning point. We wouldn't have wanted to do the commercial. People do it now because they're struggling to make money musically, now that the concept of music being available for free has been accepted. Back then we could make money in other ways, we could support ourselves, so we didn't need to [do commercials]."

****

Going back to when we used to pay for music then, what was the first single you ever bought?

"I bought two at the same time, and I'll tell you both and be honest," [Clark smiles at the thought of what he is about to reveal]. "One was cool and one was not. One was called 'Looking Through The Window' by The Jackson Five. It was a great record. The other was "Ernie (The Fastest Milkman In The West)" by Benny Hill. There's me sounding all arty a minute ago!"

****

And the message with "Ernie" was?

"We don't die. Our spirits persist!" [Clark laughs].

****

We are both laughing as Clark leaves to change into his stage outfit. He may have had a blip in his choice of music when he was younger, but his performance later that day was flawless.

POP QUIZ

Compiled by Alan Read

The Eighties saw fitness become part of everyday life, with daily appearances on screen from The Green Goddess (Diana Moran) and "Mad Lizzie" Webb. Time to give the old grey matter a workout now with these 30 teasing testers:

Q1. Wham!'s final single was a double A-side. 'The Edge of Heaven' was one side, what was the other?

....

Q2. Did Madness have 15, 17 or 19 Top 20 singles during the 80s?

....

Q3. Three 80's No.1s have Red in their title. What are they?

....

Q4. Which band started life as Johnny & The Self Abusers?

....

Q5. Who replaced Jay Aston when she left Bucks Fizz in 1985?

....

Q6. Deniece, Doris, Steadman and Lorraine were four of the members of 5 Star. Who was the fifth?

....

Q7. Under what name did Bruce Robert Howard find fame in the Eighties?

....

Q8. Vaughan Toulouse was the lead singer of which 80's one hit wonder band?

....

Q9. Who wrote Dexys' 1982 hit 'Jackie Wilson Said'?

....

Q10. The Creatures was a splinter group from which band?

....

Q11. 'Let It All Blow' was a hit in 1984 for which band?

....

Q12. Who released the album 'Like Gangbusters' in 1983?

....

Q13. How many of the 'Now That's What I Call Music' series were released in the Eighties?

....

Q14. Which song connects The Belle Stars & Natasha?

....

Q15. What is the connection between 'There Must Be An Angel' by Eurythmics, 'I Feel For You' by Chaka Khan and 'I Guess That's Why They Call It The Blues' by Elton John?

....

Q16. Who is the only artist to win Best British Male at the Brits more than once during the Eighties?

....

Q17. "I want to drown my sorrow, no tomorrow, no tomorrow" is a line from which 80's hit?

....

Q18. Who sang the theme to the Bond movie 'Licence To Kill'?

....

Q19. Which was the first band of the Eighties to enter the charts at Number 1?

....

Q20. Which 80's single has the distinction of being the 500th UK No.1?

....

Q21. Who had a hit with 'French Kiss' in 1989?

....

Q22. Which 80's No.1 was the first to be written, produced, arranged and performed by the same person?

....

Q23. Which album did Rolling Stone magazine vote Best of The 80s?

....

Q24. Whose first and last 80's hits were 'A Forest' and 'Love Song'?

....

Q25. Same title, different song: Which track was a Top 20 hit for both Genesis and Dead Or Alive?

....

Q26. Which Madonna hit came from the soundtrack of the movie 'Vision Quest'?

....

Q27. Who sings the first line on Band Aid II's 1989 version of 'Do They Know It's Christmas'?

....

Q28. Whose 80's albums include 'British Steel' and 'Screaming For Vengeance'?

....

Q29. What was Holly Johnson's debut solo single?

....

Q30. Which reflective 1980 single was the UK's first digitally recorded hit?

....

20 Questions with...

Musical Youth's Dennis Seaton

Musical Youth spent three weeks at the top of the UK charts in October 1982, with their debut single 'Pass The Dutchie'. The band enjoyed subsequent success with the singles 'Youth of Today', 'Never Gonna Give You Up', and collaborated on Donna Summer's 1983 Top 20 hit 'Unconditional Love'.

A member of Musical Youth since 1981, Dennis Seaton continues to front the Brummie reggae band, which includes his son Theo on trumpet, and original member Michael Grant on keyboards. Dennis took a break from stealing apple pies to answer 20 quick-fire questions:

****

1. What is your favourite 80's song?
Good Thing Going by Sugar Minott.

****

2. What was the best 80's TV programme?
Grange Hill.

****

3. Who was your teenage crush?
Deniece Williams.

****

4. What was your favourite subject at school?
Maths.

****

5. What job would you have done if you hadn't been a singer?
Electrician.

****

6. What do you miss most about the Eighties?
Blues parties.

****

7. What was the first single you ever bought?
Couldn't afford singles so we taped off the radio.

****

8. Where did you perform your first gig?
Casablanca Club, Cardiff.

****

9. Where is the best place you have ever visited?
New York.

****

10. Which five people, living or dead, would be your ideal dinner guests?
Bob Marley, Nelson Mandela, Barack Obama, John Barnes and Stevie Wonder.

****

11. Who is the most famous person you have ever met?
Michael Jackson.

****

12. Which pet hate would you consign to Room 101?
Dog owners who let their dogs poo on the street and in parks where children play.

****

13. What makes you angry?
Racism in society.

****

14. What is the last book you read?
Amy Winehouse and the 27 Club by Howard Sounes.

****

15. What are you most proud of?
My family.

****

16. What would be your perfect day?
Winning the lottery.

****

17. What is the best Christmas present you've ever had?
Every Christmas with my family.

****

18. And the worst?
When I was eight years old my mum was in Nevis with my sister for Christmas.

****

19. What do you want for Christmas this year?
Haven't thought that far ahead yet, but I guess health and happiness would be a good start.

****

20. What are your hopes for the future?
To be able to perform as long as possible and record as many albums as possible.

1984 That was the year...

Apple released the Macintosh computer
Introduced on 24th January, the first Apple Mac went on sale with a price tag of $2,495. Featuring an 8 MHz processor and 128K RAM, each computer was given a personal touch and signed by those involved in its making, including Steve Jobs.

****

Macca made it alone
Paul McCartney achieved his only entirely solo No. 1 single, when 'Pipes of Peace' spent two weeks topping the charts in January.

****

Torvill & Dean skated to success
The Zetra Stadium in Sarajevo, Yugoslavia was the backdrop for the pair's Olympic gold skating. Their performance to Ravel's Bolero, on 14th February, saw the couple receive maximum points and a standing ovation from the 8,500 spectators.

****

Halfpennies had it
Nigel Lawson announced the imminent demise of the ½p coin on 1st February. The littlest copper was finally withdrawn from circulation on 31st December.

****

PC Yvonne Fletcher was shot
The police officer suffered fatal injuries during a demonstration outside the Libyan Embassy in London, on 17th April. The 25-year-old was shot from inside the embassy, as gunfire opened on the demonstrating anti-Gaddafi supporters.

****

The Thames Barrier opened
Fully operational since 1982, the flood defence system was officially opened by Queen Elizabeth II on 8th May. Based on a concept devised by Reginald Charles Draper, the barrier cost over £500 million to build.

****

Tetris was released
The first video game to come out of the USSR, Tetris was the brainchild of Russian computer engineer and game designer Alexey Pajitnov. Released in the Soviet Union on 6th June, the game became available in the West in 1986.

****

BBC's Rock Around The Clock
Hosted by David Hepworth, Mark Ellen, Steve Blacknell, and Richard Skinner, the 15 hour long programme began broadcasting on the afternoon of 25th August. The music marathon included performances by New Order, The Cure, Simple Minds and The Pretenders, a 'Rockalikes' contest, and viewers voting for their choice of videos to be played.

****

Brighton was bombed
In an attempt to assassinate Margaret Thatcher, the IRA exploded a long-delay time bomb at the city's Grand Hotel, during the Conservative Party conference. The blast tore through the middle of the building in the early hours of 12th October, killing 5 and injuring 31 people.

****

Band Aid recorded 'Do They Know It's Christmas?'
More than thirty musicians gathered at London's Sarm Studios on 25th November, to record the ground-breaking charity single, written by Bob Geldof and Midge Ure. Selling a million copies in the first week of its release, the single raised over £8 million during the following year.

****

We said a final goodbye to:
Bernard Youens, Diana Dors, Eric Morecambe, Jackie Wilson, James Mason, Johnny Weissmuller, Lennard Pearce, Leonard Rossiter, Marvin Gaye, Richard Burton and Tommy Cooper.

UK Chart Toppers included:

Frankie Goes To Hollywood -Relax, Two Tribes and The Power of Love

Wham!
- Wake Me Up Before You Go Go and Freedom

George Michael
- Careless Whisper

Chaka Khan
- I Feel For You

Lionel Richie
- Hello

Duran Duran
- The Reflex

Stevie Wonder
- I Just Called To Say I Love You.

Top Films included:

Indiana Jones & The Temple of Doom,
Footloose,
Ghostbusters,
Beverly Hills Cop,
Gremlins,
Nineteen Eighty-Four,
The Terminator,
Purple Rain, Dune,
The Karate Kid,
Romancing The Stone,
This is Spinal Tap,
Splash, Against All Odds,
Police Academy,
The Killing Fields,
and Oxford Blues.

****

Rear of The Year:
Elaine Paige

Festival Days

One of the great advantages of the increasing popularity of 80's music, is the growing number of retro festivals taking place throughout the summer months. Whether it is a small, local affair or one of the more established events, there are some certainties: there will be plenty of neon, at least one of the songs performed will make you look back wistfully at your youth, you will encounter various lookalikes (usually Adam Ant and Michael Jackson) throughout the day, the weather will catch you out somehow (sunburn, a soaking or both), and you will have some of the best fun of your adult life.

Let's Rock Birmingham was one of the first such festivals of 2016. Held at Sandwell Valley Country Park on 11th June, it was the first time the festival had visited the Midlands. If audience reaction and comments are anything to go by, it should become a permanent addition to the Let's Rock family, whose other locations include Leeds, Southampton, London, Bristol, Exeter and Cookham, home to the initial Let's Rock The Moor. I spoke to festival newbie Marnie Richards about her thoughts on the day:

"Let's Rock [Birmingham] was my first 80's festival and I definitely have caught the bug to want to go to more. Such a great atmosphere … chilled. All the bands were brilliant live. I loved Peter Cox singing my favourite 'Don't Look Down'."

The Go West frontman was a hit with "barrier babe" Tanya Raftery too. The 80's music fan took devotion to another level, spending more than ten hours positioned at the front of the crowd, just feet away from the stage and the day's performers. Her endurance was rewarded when her favourite duo arrived.

"My heart beat a little bit faster when Peter Cox gave us a thumbs up and a thank you for us holding up our 'Faithful' poster. [I] love the guys' performance, the music and the love they give their faithful Westie fans."

I can understand wanting to be near the stage when a favourite act is playing, but what drives a person stay there throughout the entire day?

"For me, it's that being right up there with the band, living the music with them as they sing and play. I love watching their facial expressions and moves. It makes the event more of an intimate one and you do, of course, have the opportunity to interact more with the bands. I feel totally drawn into a performance when I'm a barrier babe, no crush in the crowd, no distractions in front of me. I can fully take in every aspect of the performance. It's a thrilling experience, and you can get some amazing action photos, to evoke wonderful memories after the event."

Having captured a number of 80's acts' great live performance moments, some of which appear in this publication, I wondered if Tanya had entailed any drawbacks in her dedication obtaining such images.

"I do think you miss out on that whole 'festival experience' and you miss some of the mad capers of other festival goers

Peter Cox

Deniece Pearson, Five Star

that go on at the back of the crowd. I never drink alcohol [during the show] and take in little other refreshment, as I never want to miss a moment of the music because I had to pop to the toilet."

I'm not sure I could find that level of discipline myself. I enjoyed standing at the front to see Dr. & The Medics kick off proceedings with a loud and lively set, giving no hint of the fact they had been drinking in the hotel bar only hours beforehand. A fact I know to be true because I was with them and had the sore head to prove it! However, once Clive and the band had finished

their set I made my way to the seated area, where we had parked our chairs and essential ephemera: brolly (sporadically in use), suntan lotion (wishful thinking) and extra layers of clothing (practicality over style).

I headed back to the stage to see various performances, including Tiffany's long overdue return to the UK and a highly polished song and dance set by Five Star. The irony of the day's first shower starting as they were singing 'Rain or Shine' was not lost on me. I was also there for headlining act Holly Johnson, not only for a better view and some close-up shots. Experience has

taught me that when it gets a bit chilly, as it had done a couple of hours earlier, the best place to be is in amongst the crowd. Having warmed up on the body heat surrounding me, I made my way to the far end of the field for a spectacular view of a crimson-lit stage, as the former Frankie Goes To Hollywood frontman gave his first live performance of 'Ascension', his contribution to the Fly album, released in March this year. I could not have envisaged a better scenario as the evening drew to an end.

My meanderings around the park throughout the performances were

Festival Days

made easier by my lack of stature. I've found people tend to be happy to let me through the crowd, or even stand in front of them, when I only come up to their chest (I should add at this point, I'm not actually a Munchkin but at 5ft 1" it's easy to lose me in a crowd!). However, my experience was in stark contrast to Tanya's:

"People often think because you are short, they can easily intimidate you or push you away from the barrier. Well, I hate to disappoint, but this barrier babe always finds the strength and has the determination to remain at the spot she earned fairly, right from the start of the day."

Feisty talk, and a reminder of an incident in the V.I.P. area at last year's Rewind South that, as well as being a victory for us shorties, goes to prove that money does not buy good manners. It was early evening and, in need of an energy boost, I had left the enclosure to buy a snack. Returning about 20 minutes later, box of churros in hand, to where my friend was sitting I was surprised to see a small group of people stood directly in front of her and my empty seat, obliterating her view of the stage. Brushing against a bare, white hairy leg as I sat down (bearing a close resemblance to Christopher Biggins had not stopped the guy standing incredibly close to my deckchair dressing like George Michael in the Wake Me Up Before You Go Go video) I asked my friend what was going on. She explained that shortly after my departure, these people had come and stood in the "gap" where my unoccupied seat was, and soon drifted in front of her too. Giving them the benefit of the doubt they were unaware of the obstruction they were causing, I stood up and asked the group to move. All but Mr. Choose Life, who dwarfed me in both girth and in height, did so straight away. He told me he wasn't budging, I shouldn't have left my seat if I didn't want someone to stand in front of it, and then turned back to face the stage.

Keeping in check my desire to throttle this guy who seemed hell bent on causing trouble, I looked around to see if Security was nearby. As I did so, one of the guys sat to the right of me got up and told the Wham! wannabe to stop being ignorant, and to get out of the way. This was swiftly followed by a Scotsman to my left doing the same, but in far more colourful language. Then, in a scene reminiscent of the film Spartacus, people started jumping up out of their seats from the rows behind and in front too, backing up my assertion that he should move. Realising when he was beaten, and with his mates having long deserted him, my antagonist made a quick exit, leaving me with a deep gratitude towards my neighbouring festival-goers.

Will Mellor

48

Mike Read

I have to stress that this is the only time I have ever known such boorish behaviour at a festival. The willingness of so many people to get involved in remedying the situation, illustrates the rarity of such occurrences, and most peoples' inclination is to enhance others' enjoyment, rather than spoil it. Random conversations whilst queuing for the toilets, a spontaneous duet with a passer-by, or ad hoc dancing with a stranger are what make these events memorable. That sense of camaraderie extends to those on stage too.

One festival performance that remains firmly in mind is The Boomtown Rats' set at Rewind South in 2014. An avid Rats fan, I stood feet away from the stage; close enough to detect every expression and nuance from Bob and the boys. However, even those farthest away from the band were left in no doubt of a father's grief, during the performance of "I Don't Like Mondays". The long pause as the Irishman looked out over the audience, having just sung the line "and the lesson today is how to die" only months after losing daughter Peaches, was incredibly moving. Apparently lost in private thought in front of a crowd of thousands, the singer momentarily dropped the Bobby Boomtown façade with which we are so familiar. A lone shout of "We love you, Bob" broke the silence, setting off a wave of similar cries of affection throughout the

gathered throng. At that point in time, we were as one.

Then, there are those special solitary moments. A few perfect minutes when the masses fade away, and it's just you and a favourite song being sung live by a musical hero of adolescence. A time when all is right with the world. You never know who you might meet at a festival either. At last year's Rewind South, I turned around and was pleasantly surprised to find Will Mellor stood behind me. I was still beaming from the encounter when I bumped into Mike Read a short time later. Sporting an original Radio 1 Roadshow shirt, the DJ was unaware of how much willpower it took for me to refrain from bursting into a chorus of "Mike Read, Mike Read, 275 and 285". Well, it is what Smiley Miley had encouraged us to do over thirty years previously, during the roadshow's visit to the South Coast.

Having experienced a number of the retro festivals on offer on the UK mainland, I was delighted to be invited to this year's Jack Up The 80s Festival on the Isle of Wight. Now in its fourth year of operation, the event is held in beautiful countryside just outside of Newchurch. When I arrived there on Saturday morning, the sky was blue, the sun was shining, and the gathering crowds were in good spirits.

As local bands High School Never Ends and Ska'd For Life began proceedings, I wandered around chatting to some of the festival-goers.

The brightly adorned bunch pictured below were eagerly anticipating the 80's acts due on stage later that day. A girl after my own heart, Tracie was looking forward to seeing Paul Young, whereas both Jackie and Denise had set their sights on Leo Sayer. It was Johnny Hates Jazz who Louise had come to see and, as I was photographing the band during their performance, I felt someone tap me on the shoulder. It was Louise, smiling from ear to ear and loving every minute of the show.

Throughout the entire day, and indeed the weekend, the keyword was 'fun'. From the pitch perfect performance of Londonbeat to the legendary Leo Sayer, the festival was about much more than the superb standard and diversity of music it offered. More than any other retro event I have attended, Jack Up The 80s had a happy, relaxed vibe which reached across the generations. Dawn (a former Brosette) and Alex are from the island, and were attending the festival for the first time, along with Dawn's son Pietro and Alex's daughter Imogen. Both mums were impressed with how family friendly the day was, remarking that it was perfect for children "who love singing and dancing".

L-R: Jackie, Denise, Louise and Tracie

Festival Days

L-R Imogen, Pietro, Alex, Dawn

80's music fans Phil (left) and Bruce

I think you would have been hard pushed to find anyone there who didn't love to sing and dance, including a number of twenty-somethings. Phil (22) and Bruce (23) were working at the festival but are also big fans of 80's music.

I asked if they shared the true 80's passion for buying vinyl. "No, that's a hipster sort of thing," replied Bruce (I guess that must make me a hipster!). A fan of The Jam, he was keen to see his namesake perform later that day. When Mr. Foxton did come on stage, the long held secret behind his musical genius was at last revealed. As the photograph shows, he is in fact a Jedi knight! At least that explains how he is able to perform with as much energy as he did four decades ago. From start to finish, there was an inimitable dynamism running throughout From The Jam's set, epitomised by Bruce's famous mid-

air jump. Outstanding on many levels, the band's performance was my highlight of the weekend.

For dancer Lucy Bowdery, the weekend had looked set to be a disappointment. Her plans to dance alongside some of the acts on Saturday went awry when her dancing partner failed to show. The 29-year-old from Shanklin told me it is not the first time her festival work has been without incident. When Blondie appeared at the Isle of Wight Festival in 2013, Lucy says "I was working as a fairy when I accidentally trapped her [Debbie Harry] in a portaloo. Blondie was trying to get by and my wings were blocking her in!"

Lucy Bowdery

Fortunately, Lucy's partner turned up on Sunday, and the pair danced on stage alongside Brother Beyond's Nathan Moore and then Owen Paul. It seems incredible that it is thirty years since the Glaswegian singer released his No. 3 hit single "My Favourite Waste of Time". It is also three decades since Five Star, another of the day's fantastic acts, released their most successful single, the No. 2 hit 'Rain Or Shine'. Perhaps even more unbelievable is the fact that Sunday's headliners, Bad Manners, celebrate their 40th anniversary this year.

During a high octane set which, as well as hits such as 'Lip Up Fatty', 'Just A Feeling', 'Lorraine' and 'Special Brew', included ska favourites 'Feel Like Jumping' and 'Fatty Fatty', Buster and the boys bounced, danced and ran around the stage, having a blast - everything we have come to expect from a Bad Manners gig.

However, the accolade for Star of The Weekend must go to Leo Sayer. I first became aware of the singer's arrival during Johnny Hates Jazz's set. I had gone backstage to jot down a few notes, and was singing along to 'Turn Back The Clock', when I felt someone brush past me. It was the pocket rocket singer himself. Very soon there was a buzz in the air, as word of his presence got around. Everyone wanted to meet the man who had brought us hits such as 'Have You Ever Been In Love', 'When I Need You' and 'You Make Me Feel Like Dancing', and everyone did. A true gentleman of pop, the one man band left people feeling as if he was as pleased to meet them as they were him. He then went on to deliver an electrifying performance of tracks spanning four decades. All I know is, anyone who can make Bruce Foxton dance the way Leo Sayer did, gets the thumbs up from me.

I can honestly say that Jack Up The 80s is the best retro festival I have been to, and recommend everyone descends upon the Isle of Wight next August for Volume 5. Overleaf are a few more photos to show just how fabulous the weekend was.

Leo Sayer

Bruce Foxton and From The Jam drummer Mike Randon sidestage dancing to Leo Sayer

Festival Days Photos

From The Jam

Paul Young

Paul Young

Bruce Foxton and Paul Young

Leo Sayer

Bad Manners

Buster Bloodvessel

Londonbeat

Bubbles!

Stedman and Delroy, Five Star

Five Star

THAT'S ENTERTAINMENT

Releasing 18 consecutive UK Top 40 hits between 1977 and the end of 1982, The Jam made a huge impact not only on the charts but on a generation of music lovers. Little wonder then that when Rick Buckler put together The Gift in 2006 to play The Jam's material, it was met with a warm welcome.

The band also included Russell Hastings and David Moore. In 2007, Bruce Foxton joined the group, at which point the name was changed to From The Jam.

Touring prolifically and recording the albums 'Back In The Room' and 'Smash The Clock' (released as Bruce Foxton, and featuring Paul Weller playing on some tracks), From The Jam continue to keep the music and Mod culture alive. Having previously included Big Country's Mark Brzezicki on drums, the band's current line-up comprises of Bruce Foxton (Bass), Russell Hastings (Guitar/Lead Vocals), Mike Randon (Drums) and Andy Fairclough (Hammond Organ).

I caught up with Bruce Foxton and Russell Hastings shortly after they had finished their set at the Jack Up The 80s festival.

How does performing today compare with back in the Eighties?
Bruce: "Well, I think we're better at it! Festivals and The Jam ... it's not something we've ever been that comfortable with. It's a learning curve, and I think it's taken us this long to get it right. It's a different environment to being in a theatre, playing to however many's here today, so you've got to try and work at it."

Have you got a favourite track you like to perform?
Russell: "No, that changes daily. It changes all the time. Strange Town's a

great track. We didn't play it tonight. They're all great tracks, but sometimes I'll dig my teeth into something and think 'Yeah, great'."
Bruce: "It changes day to day, and from gig to gig really. It's an easy out, but I love playing them all."

So, what did you enjoy playing most today?
Bruce: "Well, just the whole gig ... I think it's been fantastic. Beat Surrender, we haven't played that for a while, so it's kinda like fresh because it's had a bit of a rest. A lot of songs have been in the set for a while, so it was good to play it."

How do the retro festivals compare with From The Jam gigs?
Russell: "They're slightly different, they're less intense ... happier. They're sort of easier in a way because not everyone out there has come to see us, so you've just got to go out there and do what you do, to try and win everybody over because they've come to see other people as well. At our gigs, they've come to see us and you've got to live up to something. Do you know what I mean? We can have a lot of fun at these, 'cause the sun's out. We have a lot of fun at the festivals. They're good."

You were a big fan of The Jam, Russell, so how does it feel to be fronting From The Jam?
Russell: "It's incredible ... such great songs. The energy of the songs, I think that never dies. I've been doing it for ten or twelve years, something like that, but it's always exciting ... and we're very fortunate ... me and Bruce often say ... you know, we're outside Sydney Opera House and we're having dinner out there ... we are dead lucky. Or we're on Bondai Beach or in New York or Singapore, Abu Dhabi, Dubai ... it's great, really good. Tonight's been a real buzz as well."

To be accepted by The Jam's fans must have felt good?

Russell: "Absolutely, really good from the beginning. They were really kind to me right from day one."

Why do you think The Jam's music has endured?
Bruce: "I think they're great songs. I know that sounds conceited, doesn't it really? I just think they're great songs, they've stood the test of time. You hear them on the radio, they still sound fantastic. We had something to say, the lyrics were good ... they meant something to a lot of people, and I think that's why."
Russell: "Because they were fantastic songs [that had] the energy of the time ... and politically I think there was a lot going on at the time. There was a hell of a lot going on really, and Paul [Weller] was very clever with his lyrics, but he didn't feel like he was clever, you know. I spoke to Paul about his lyrics ... we've spoken many times about that sort of stuff. Paul sang about everybody's day-to-day lives, and then people identified with it and the band. The Jam sang about people's lives ... Saturday's kids, council houses, V-neck shirts, baggy trousers and so on. Going Underground with all the rockets and guns, and Eton Rifles with what was going on with the Tories and the Labour Party. Also, they were great at writing amazing, lovely tunes that people felt ... and I think it's been a long time since a band's come along and done that sort of thing."

What was the first record you ever bought?
Russell: "Ob-la-di Ob-la-da. [Marmalade]"
Bruce: "Dave Edmunds, I think ... I Hear You Knocking. Only 'cause I really liked the radio kind of miked voice that Dave Edmunds had. It's just an effect really, but I hadn't heard vocals like that [Bruce then sings part of the song] ... "you went away and left me long time ago" ... That was a good song."

Bruce Foxton

Russell Hastings

Who were your musical influences?
Bruce: "Probably a lot of Motown, The Beatles, obviously The Who … and bands like Dr Feelgood."

Is there anything you miss about the Eighties?
Bruce: "No, I'm just living for the day, you know. I mean, I'm that much older now and a lot of things happen to you in life … the ups and downs … but, touch wood, we're enjoying it now so don't look backwards."

1985 That was the year...

Sinclair C5 launched

The brainchild of Sir Clive Sinclair, the battery-powered tricycle was launched on 10th January. Developed as an alternative form of transport for commuters, the C5 failed to achieve commercial success, but can now boast of cult status.

****

Miners returned to work

Almost a year after it began, with a walkout at Cortonwood Colliery, the Miners' Strike ended on 3rd March. The bitter trade union dispute affected thousands of families, and left shattered communities up and down the country. The defeat of the NUM (National Union of Mineworkers) greatly diminished the power of the trade union movement, ultimately changing the face of British politics.

****

Live Aid concert

The show that rocked the world began at midday on 13th July, when Status Quo kicked off proceedings at Wembley Stadium. The dual venue event included performances at JFK Stadium, Philadelphia. Thanks to a transatlantic flight on Concorde, Phil Collins holds the unique status of having played at both sites during the fundraiser.

****

Disaster struck football

Nearing the end of the first half of a league match between Bradford City and Lincoln City, on 11th May, fire broke out at the Valley Parade Stadium. The blaze quickly took hold, claiming the lives of 56 spectators and injuring 225. Further tragedy hit football later that month on 29th May, at Belgium's Heysel Football Stadium, ahead of the European Cup Final between Liverpool and Juventus. Following hostility between both sets of fans on the terraces, Liverpool supporters breached the 'neutral zone' separating both sides. The ensuing crush, as spectators attempted to escape the fighting, led to the collapse of a concrete retaining wall. More than 600 people were injured and 39 killed in what many at the time considered to be football's darkest hour. The disaster led to UEFA banning English clubs from European competition.

****

Route 66 closed

One of America's original highways, the famous 'Mother Road' running from Chicago to California was established in 1926. The emergence of the Interstate, coupled with high maintenance costs, saw the iconic route being decommissioned on 27th June.

****

Gorbachev headed the Soviet Union

Following the death of Konstantin Chernenko, Mikhail Gorbachev was elected by the Politburo to take over leadership of the USSR. His policies of glasnost (openness) and perestroika (restructuring) resulted in change within the communist country, and improvement with its relationship with the West, eventually leading to the end of the Cold War.

****

Rainbow Warrior was sunk

As Greenpeace's flagship made its way to Morura, the site of planned French nuclear testing, it exploded off the coast of Auckland, New Zealand. The cause of the explosion, on 10th June, was found to be two limpet bombs planted under the vessel by French Intelligence Service agents. They were later found guilty of the manslaughter of photographer Fernando Pereira, who had been below deck and drowned in the ensuing flooding.

****

Garry Kasparov triumphed

The Russian Grandmaster became the youngest ever player to hold the title of World Chess

Champion when, at the age of 22, he beat reigning champion Anatoly Karpov on 9th November.

****

Microsoft Windows 1.0 released

The first ever version of the software was launched, as a device driver for MS-DOS, on 20th November.

****

We said a final goodbye to:

Gary Holton, Laura Ashley, Noele Gordon, Orson Welles, Rock Hudson, Wilfred Brambell and Yul Brynner.

****

UK Chart Toppers included:

Paul Hardcastle
- 19

Madonna
- Into The Groove

Sister Sledge
- Frankie

Philip Bailey & Phil Collins
- Easy Lover

Elaine Paige & Barbara Dickson
- I Know Him So Well

Jennifer Rush
- The Power of Love

Midge Ure
- If I Was

Feargal Sharkey
- A Good Heart.

****

Top Films included:

My Beautiful Laundrette, Back To The Future, Teen Wolf, Out of Africa, Desperately Seeking Susan, The Jewel of The Nile, Cocoon, Letter To Brezhnev, Commando, A Room With A View, The Goonies, The Breakfast Club, St. Elmo's Fire, A View To A Kill, Rocky IV, and The Color Purple.

****

Rear of The Year:

Lynsey De Paul

SECRET 80's DIARY

The Untrendy Teenager's Thoughts on...

Television, Top of The Pops and The Charts

20th January, 1984
Watched Grange Hill. Jeremy's dead! He got drowned after messing about in the swimming pool. It was quite shocking and poor Zammo looked distraught at the end. Felt sorry for Mr Baxter too.

24th March
Watched Fraggle Rock. It was good. Can't wait 'til next week. It's the best programme on telly. So are Shroud For A Nightingale, Dr Who and It Ain't Half Hot Mum. Love the bit at the end where one of the Indian men is singing 'Land of hope and glory, mother of the free' and then the Sergeant Major shouts: "SHUT UPPPPPPP!!!!"

9th August
Saw TOTP. Frankie were, I think, having a bit of a laugh this week because Ped and Mark had swapped places. Holly went into the crowd and this stupid tart was hanging round him. Still, it won't do her any good. Ped and Mark were dancing back to back and trying not to laugh. It was really good. Holly also tore up a copy of The Sun, which was ace.

30th August
TOTP included Depeche Mode with Master And Servant, which is ace

(Dave Gahan was wiggling his bum like nobody's business) and The Smiths. Their song is called – wait for it – William It Was Really Nothing. I ask you! Morrissey didn't have a tree growing out of his pocket this time, but at one point he bared his chest (?!) on which was written MARRY ME. No, thanks! After that, Mike Smith did the same and it said WE LOVE THE SMITHS! Huh!

19th September
Black Adder is the 2nd best programme I've ever seen – after The Young Ones, of course. Even Mum and Dad like it. In the Letters page of Smash Hits, someone fancied Rowan Atkinson.

11th October
Oh dear, I'm depressed about Black Adder ending. I don't even have a pic of Rowan. If I had a video, I'd always save one episode of The Young Ones and Black Adder.

20th November
That silly cow Chaka Khan is still No. 1 and D'ran have dropped to No. 3. Oh Chaka, how dare you? Still, Limahl has gone up to 4, and Nik to 5. Lots of new entries, including Nick Heyward and TINA TURNER! Any chart with her in was bound to be bad.

4th December
I'm nearly crying as I write this. Why? The charts. Frankie have done it. The Power of Love is No 1. I'm so emotional right now! Other chart positions: Limahl 10, Duran 19. Although Frankie may not be there long, at least they've got their three No. 1s. Band Aid, rather surprisingly, haven't made it yet. Also, a danger is Paul Macca's one, which is up to 9 from 39. But I still think Band Aid will do it.

11th December
The telly is being hit by interferences which completely spoiled Whistle Test, which had Tony Hadley, Gary Kemp, Andy and Roger on talking about Band Aid. Yes folks, you've guessed it – it's No. 1 by miles, has broken just about every record and is completely FAB. About the only record I wouldn't mind pushing Frankie off. Actually, Frankie are No. 3. New entry at No. 2 is Wham! This had better not be No. 1. I do like Wham! but they don't deserve another one yet. The song is ACE but I'd much rather have Band Aid for Christmas No. 1 as it's such a good cause. Also, all the pop stars were friendly – typical for the Season of Goodwill.

5th February, 1985

The charts are complete CRAP. Prince is down to 5, Ghostbusters to 25, Foreigner to 3, and yes folks, you guessed it, No. 1 is Elaine Paige and Barbara Dickson! This is the final cruel blow. However, there is a new entry from Howard Jones, which has redeemed it a bit, but honestly, having I Know Him So Well for my birthday No. 1! At least Foreigner could have hung on!

19th February

Tremendous excitement! The much talked about EastEnders starts tonight. People have been going on about it all day. I'm watching it, especially as there's a boy on the front cover of the Radio Times who looks just like Damon! [from Brookside – this turned out to be Ian Beale] LATER: Watched EastEnders. It's ACE! Perhaps it won't be as big as Corrie or Brookside (not Brookside, anyway) but ace. I like one called Ali, but his wife Sue is a cow.

24th February

Spitting Image was ace. There's been a row over whether to show a puppet of the Queen Mother. At the end, Spitting Image said they didn't make one and denied everything, then suddenly one popped up and said, "Oh, what a pity! I was SO looking forward to it!"

10th April

Got up and looked to see if the new charts were on Teletext yet but they weren't, so I watched Battle of The Planets, which was quite funny as there was that stupid robot 7-Zark-7 pacing up and down. At that point, Auntie Pam popped her head round the door and exclaimed, "Ah, I see you're getting your morning dose of culture!"

7th July

I'm not watching any more Wimbledon. It's too nerve racking! Boris, who I'm developing a massive crush on, has made history by winning the first set 6-4, but was 1-0 down in the second set.
4.50pm: BORIS IS UP 2 SETS TO 1.
5.23pm: Boris has just been at championship point and lost. I could kill him!
5.40pm: History has been made! YES, BORIS WON! 6-4, 6-7, 7-6, 6-4! I just cried! It's like a fairytale. I can't even think straight. Well done, mein Liebling!

6th October

Record to watch out for: Take On Me by A-Ha (a very dishy Norway group).

5th November

Ros and I are seriously considering giving up on the charts. Well, Echo & The Bunnymen going down could be lived with, but Jennifer Rush at No. 1 for the FIFTH WEEK is rather a lot worse – but there's worse! – ARCADIA ARE DOWN TO 10! It can't be right.

17th July, 1985

Why did this have to happen to Bobby? Just as he and Pam were getting back together! Katherine is a bitch and I hope she suffered before she died. Everyone, including JR, was crying round the bed. Bobby was sobbing 'Look after Christopher and Charlie. I love you all.' Miss Ellie fell into Clayton's arms, Donna and Ray patched up their marriage at once by just crying on each other. Tears were running down JR's face as he cried 'Bobby, don't leave me!' Then the machine showing heartbeats went in a straight line. Everyone went "No, NO!" but he was dead.

3rd October

In EastEnders they kept the suspense really well, even though all the papers had said it already. Michelle phoned someone, then it just happened that Den, Ali, Tony and Andy all got phone calls. They also all set off somewhere at the same time. Anyway, Michelle was waiting, this pair of feet got out of the car and opened the back door… to let out Roly the dog. The papers were, for once, right. It was Den. They talked for a while and agreed that she should keep the baby. I felt really sorry for Den. He was almost in tears when he walked away.

9th December

Ethel from EastEnders was on Wogan

tonight, plus Willie the pug, who I now totally regret not putting for my 'Most Very Horrible Thing' in the Smash Hits poll.

22nd December

What I must say right now is that I've just realised that it's our first Christmas with the EastEnders, and they're all really festive! I watched the repeat. There were loads of carol singers, and Den got in a right mood and threatened to cancel Christmas unless the Queen Vic till thief was found. Then he went out and shouted at the carol singers, who ignored him, and it ended with one of those looks that only he can do. In spite of all this, I have a shock announcement – I think I'm in love with him! He's just so funny. I still like Ali best, but Den is ACE! Meanwhile, even Dot had a drink and Roly kept getting entangled in the Christmas tree. There were two close-ups of Willie. Urgh! That's enough from Albert Square for now.

Across The Pond to
Nu Shooz

Back performing live after a 25 year hiatus, and with the release of their new album 'Bag Town' earlier this year, Nu Shooz have been busy in 2016.
With performances alongside A Flock of Seagulls, Wang Chung and Cutting Crew for the U.S. 'Lost 80s Tour', in addition to a variety of gigs throughout the States, John Smith and Valerie Day took time out from touring to answer a few questions.

****

How does it feel to be back recording and performing?

Valerie: "We're having the time of our lives. The Eighties are better the second time around.

John: "There's way less stress, way more enjoyment."

****

Is there anything you miss about the 80s?

John: "One of the exciting things about the 80s was all that drum machine, sampler technology was new. So, I think we all loved how fake stuff sounded, how crisp and brittle it all sounded. We were thrilled by that. If I miss anything, I think I miss the newness of that. When that was new, it was so exciting … and there were about half as many people on Earth then, so we had the field more to ourselves.

Valerie: "I was thinking that I do miss being able to tour with our whole band. The dates we're doing are really fun. I wouldn't give them up for anything, but I always wish that we had a few more people with us on the road. Our band played so much, and we were so tight. It's hard to recreate that when you're not gigging every night. But on the other hand, I don't miss being in the tour van for 70 days at a stretch. There was no alone time!"

****

What have your gigs this year been like?

Valerie: "Really good. We're lucky that we get to do a variety of things. We're on some shows with dance acts like Lisa Lisa, Exposé and those kinds of acts, and then we're also on some tours this Fall with A Flock of Seagulls, the New Wave 80's thing. So, it's a real combination … and we have an eight piece band that we do shows around town [Portland, Oregon] with, so it's not just the hits. We get to go deeper into our catalogue and just have fun."

John: "The combination of the two is just perfect, it's great.

****

Your single 'I Can't Wait' reached Number 2 in the UK charts in 1986. Have you any plans to celebrate the 30th anniversary of its release?

Valerie: "We're celebrating all year long!"

John: "All the local media went crazy. Every TV station and newspaper came up to the house, and wanted to talk about the 30th anniversary of 'I Can't Wait' because it's sort of like winning the basketball championship or something. You know, we won the 1986 championship."

****

Were you tempted to release an updated version of the track?

Valerie: "We did an unplugged version. We recorded it in 2006 for the twentieth anniversary of the single. That version is really cool. We slowed it down, lowered the key and re-recorded it using all acoustic instruments and jazz musicians that I'd been playing with since we put Nu Shooz to bed all those years ago. We really loved how it turned out, so we made a whole record with those musicians, and new material that's called 'Pandora's Box'. That was created ten years ago, and 'Pandora's Box' was released in 2010. It's still one of our favourite projects because it's so out there, compared to all the other dance music and R&B tracks that we've done.

****

What about taking the track in the other direction, maybe with a rap or electronic sound?

John: "No, we're jazz people."

Valerie: "Mann and 50 Cent did the best job of that."

John: "Buzzin'."

Valerie: "That was one of our favourite versions ever. They took it and brought it into the 2000s, into the new century."

John: "They wrote new sections for it, and the message was really positive. It was really as good as anybody could do."

Photo Credit: Nancy Bundt

Photo Credit: Hiroshi Iwaya

Bag Town

Who are your musical influences?

John: "Really eclectic influences, from old Blues guys to Leon Russell and Carole King, and Latin guys. We started out in Latin bands, so I got really hooked on horns from playing in a Latin band. And Hendrix, of course, Coltrane, Charlie Parker, that kind of stuff. For fun, I guess Chic and Rick James.

Valerie: "Nile Rodgers we should add to that list, and Johnny 'Guitar' Watson … Aretha Franklin, Gladys Knight and Esperanza Spalding. She came out of Jazz. She's a bass player and a wonderful singer.

****

The inspiration for 'Bag Town' came when, struggling with a creative block, John idly began creating puppets from the leftover lunch bags in his studio. Before long, he had made a whole town of buildings and bag people, and the music was quick to follow.

****

Do you think fun is the key to unlocking creativity?

John: "We had so much fun making 'Bag Town', from the first note to the last it was just fun. We set out to have fun, and we did. We came to love the bag people. They got names."

Valerie: "We finally took them off the piano … and I go in the studio now and go 'Where are they?' [sighs] But we're going to bring them back for the video, and they will be immortalised even more. We're going to create an actual bag town, where we're animated within it."

****

What is your favourite track on 'Bag Town'?

Valerie: 'Your Perfect Day' is probably one of my favourite tracks. I think the background vocals on it are really beautiful, and something about it too … when things are really bad, where would you go in your imagination? What would your perfect day be? It's overwhelming sometimes, to be able to go to your perfect day in your mind.

John: "It was an actual game that we used to play. I drove my son to school every morning. It was drizzly … we'd get up and the damp was sticking knives in you, and I'd turn to him and say "So, what would your perfect day be right now?" We actually did this every day, so it was a great thing to write a song about it. My favourite tracks are 'The Real Thing', which a lot of work went into, and 'Tell Me A Lie', which I love playing live."

****

Going back to the 80s for the last question. What was your worst fashion mistake of the decade?

Valerie: "There were so many! I think the giant shoulder pads. Then, I had a friend who was a hairdresser in Beauty School. She's the one responsible for my blonde hair, which was fine, but she also tried to perm it with a cap, where you pull the hair through. It just fried the whole thing! I tried to get the brassiness out, by using this shampoo that's supposed to tone down the brassiness, but it was for brunettes not blondes. So, I turned my hair splotchy pink. I wish I had photos of it."

John: "I'm glad you don't! I always thought shoulder pads were ridiculous. You know, people were putting them in t-shirts then, and it just looked horrible. I kinda went psychedelic hippy. My worst fashion mistake, and still I'll be driving and I think of this and I just kinda shudder. If you look at what I was wearing on Top of The Pops, it's just horrible and nobody told me.

Valerie: "Was that the pink suit?"

John: "It was pink something, but the hat was all bad too …"

Valerie: "You rocked pink though, I just have to say, better than I ever did."

John: "It's not your colour." [laughs]

Valerie: "His look was always better than mine at that time."

John: "Yeah, independent. It was kinda like the Emperor's new clothes … I could see that completely sucks. Women in big football pads, you know, that's not good. My conscience is relatively clear except for Top of The Pops."

Steve Blacknell's Top 10 Music Videos

On July 13th 1985, television presenter Steve Blacknell became part of 80's pop history, when he interviewed Phil Collins. The interview took place on Concorde, during the transatlantic flight which allowed the singer to perform at both Live Aid venues; London's Wembley Stadium and John F. Kennedy Stadium, Philadelphia. Steve also has the accolade of being Europe's first VJ, so who better to tell us his favourite 80's music videos?

****

"I Ran" - A Flock of Seagulls

I saw this quirky quartet supporting Bette Bright at The Venue in London in 1981. They wore bright yellow jumpsuits and looked weird … and that hair! For no apparent reason, "I Ran" stuck out a mile and I, in turn, 'ran' to my new boss at Jive Records, raving that it was a Top Ten record in the USA. We signed them and it went to Number 9! The video is not the best in the world, but it always reminds me that you have to reach out for those special moments.

****

"Red Skies" - The Fixx

As co-host of the BBC music arts show Riverside, we had a bit of a say in getting bands on the show. I knew and adored this band from the word go, and I battled like fury to get them on the show - and eventually won! They played this on the show and, for me, the video still stands up today. The Fixx are still my favourite rock band of all time, and are still creating amazing music.

****

"Grass" - XTC

This band could and should have been the 80's Beatles. This video, in reverse motion, is pure LSD. "Laying on the grass my heart it flares like fire. The way you slap my face just fills me with desire". Andy Partridge always conducted the proceedings - a crazed cross between mad professor and reticent superstar! A true genius.

****

"Dirty Creature" - Split Enz

Despite being their record company PR man, I would follow 'The Enz' up and down the UK in my own time. Live, they're bizarre and a total revelation. My wife and I played this video non-stop. It's addictive and wonderfully put together, as well as showing a chart band in their true colours. When they split up, Tim and Neil took me for lunch, and Neil revealed his new band ... Crowded House. I stifled a laugh. 'You must be joking,' I thought. 'What a name for a band!'

****

"Heart of Lothian" – Marillion

There have been a few bands here and there who have divided their fan base, i.e. you liked early Beefheart or the later stuff. Fish and Co. were another, as in the Genesis conundrum. I loathed the latter and adored Marillion. So, I was thrilled to bits to have a cameo in this pub-based epic shoot, thrown out by Sir John Otway and Glynn Edwards from "Minder". With more eyeliner than Dusty Springfield and higher than the highest kite, I was in heaven!

****

"Once In A Lifetime" - Talking Heads

Another hero of mine, David Byrne, ascends to another level of craziness in this anarchic clip. Just him, a white screen, and a suit. I was flabbergasted when I first saw this in 1980, and was drawn into his world of absurd physicality. I would remember and duplicate his wacky ways when I got my own MTV USA show four years later, jumping and gyrating like a man possessed, while up top … a talking head!

****

"Take On Me" - A-Ha

Directed by the genial Steve Barron, this featured the then amazing new sketch technique of 'Rotoscoping'. I had to interview him for MTV at the time, and was, as many were, just amazed at its visual impact. A few weeks later, I did the band's first ever TV interview (for Children's BBC) in the lounge of my Shepherd's Bush flat. I became a huge fan, and felt positively ugly alongside them whenever we met. That pretty and that talented ... it made me sick!

****

"Hold Me Now" - The Thompson Twins

I worked with the band from the very start, as their "pet" interviewer. Although not one of the world's greatest videos, it sends me back to those wonderful times. When they got an encore at a BBC "Sight And Sound" broadcast, Tom got up and told everyone they would have to hang on a bit whilst they wound back the backing tapes, so they could sing the song again. Marvellous!

****

"Like A Hurricane" - Neil Young & Crazy Horse

This incredible 1986 version of a song released almost a decade before just sends shivers up and down my spine. The energy and intensity of the band is infectious. Having known my good lady wife for four decades, we have always differed in our musical tastes. However, we both agree that this particular version is going to be played at both our funerals. It's very, very special to us, and that searing opening guitar reduces us to pulp. Incredible.

****

"Relax" - Frankie Goes To Hollywood

My mate Bob Johnson bought the original video of this round to my seedy North London flat. He was looking after them, and I was jaw-struck! The Amazing Leather Pets were in cages above, and the band looked SO brave and crazed. I tried to get it on my BBC "Riverside" show but it was deemed too rude, so my chums on "The Tube" snapped it up. Thanks to my mucker Mike Read, it did rather well, but it has to be said, it would never have made the impact it did without the genius of Trevor Horn at the helm.

1986 That was the year...

John McCarthy was kidnapped

The 30-year-old World Wide Television News journalist was abducted by militant group Islamic Jihad, on his way to Beirut airport on 17th April. After more than five years in captivity, during which time his girlfriend Jill Morrell campaigned for his release, McCarthy was freed on 8th August 1991.

****

Chernobyl Nuclear Disaster

An explosion in one of the power plant's four nuclear reactors, in the early hours of 26th April, led to the catastrophic release of radiation, a hundred times greater than that of the Hiroshima and Nagasaki bombings. Fallout contamination, although heaviest at the Russian site, reached dangerous levels as far as Finland, Sweden and Poland.

****

World Cup controversy

Diego Maradona scored twice for Argentina during their quarter final match against England, on 22nd June. The 2-1 final result, which included the South American midfielder's controversial "Hand of God" goal, saw England knocked out of the World Cup.

****

Prince Andrew married Sarah Ferguson

The Queen's second son wed his flame-haired bride at Westminster Abbey on 26th June. Despite the lack of "fairytale" spin given to his elder brother's wedding five years earlier, Andrew's nuptials still drew a worldwide television audience of 500 million.

****

Bob Geldof & Paula Yates wed

After a decade together, the pair were married in Las Vegas on 31st August. The marriage was later blessed in a star-studded ceremony in October, held at their Davington Priory home. The bride wore a red satin and velvet dress created by fashion designer, and godfather to her daughter Fifi Trixibelle, Jasper Conran.

****

Desmond Tutu made history

One of South Africa's leading opponents of apartheid, the bishop became the country's first black person to head the Anglican Church, when he assumed the position of Archbishop of Cape Town, on 7th September.

****

The M25 was completed

Work on the 117 mile London Orbital Motorway had first begun in the early Seventies, with sections of the route opening as construction was completed. The last stretch of the motorway, between Micklefield and South Mimms, was officially opened by Margaret Thatcher on 29th October.

****

Mike Tyson beat Trevor Berbick

Billed as Judgment Day, the fight on 22nd November saw Tyson beat the current Heavyweight Champion of the World in a technical knockout. The win resulted in the 20-year-old boxer becoming the youngest ever competitor to hold the title.

****

We said a final goodbye to:

Benny Goodman, Cary Grant, Dustin Gee, Harold MacMillan, James Cagney, Pat Phoenix, Phil Lynott and Wallis Simpson.

****

UK Chart Toppers included:

George Michael
- A Different Corner,
Chris De Burgh
- Lady In Red,

Berlin
- Take My Breath Away,
Wham!
- Edge of Heaven,
Madonna
- Papa Don't Preach and True Blue,
Diana Ross
- Chain Reaction,
Boris Gardiner
- I Want To Wake Up With You,
and Dr. & The Medics
- Spirit In The Sky.

****

Top Films included:
Top Gun, Pretty In Pink,
Stand By Me, Absolute Beginners,
Clockwise, Aliens,
Ferris Bueller's Day Off,
Flight of the Navigator,
Platoon, The Fly,
The Golden Child,
9½ Weeks,
The Mission, Labyrinth,
Crocodile Dundee, Cobra,
The Color of Money,
and When The Wind Blows.

****

Rear of The Year:
Anneka Rice & Michael
Barrymore

There's a Guy works down the Berni, swears he's Andrew....

An 80's short story by Jo Bartlett

'I'm telling you, he's a dead ringer for Andrew. You've got to trust me, having dinner at the Berni Inn will change your life!' Cherry shot me a look from under her fringe, it was so long the Brownies could probably have borrowed it for a camp out. Still, despite taking her at least twenty minutes to perfect every morning, I had to admit she was starting to look like Susanne Sulley from The Human League, which was her ultimate ambition in life.

'And by Andrew, I take it you mean Andrew Ridgeley? Not that Andy Johnson from the upper sixth, whose eyebrows meet in the middle and make him look like a serial killer.'

'Of course I mean Andrew Ridgeley, Janey. Your Andrew. I swear the waiter couldn't have looked more like him if they were twins.' Cherry grinned, her mouth heavily coated in the new lip gloss she'd just bought from Miss Selfridge. Looking down at my outfit from C&A, I sighed. Cherry was wearing a neon ra-ra skirt from Snob, and she had a monthly clothing allowance which she got to spend however she liked. Unlike me, who only got to buy clothes with my mother in tow, when she'd

suggest things like just slipping on the trousers for size in the shop, as no-one was looking and the queue for the changing rooms was far too long. Cherry had no idea how lucky she was.

'But how am I ever going to persuade my mum and dad to go to the Berni Inn?' I bit my lip, it was all right for Cherry. Her mum's new boyfriend, Tony, was always taking them to places like that, at least when Cherry was home. She stayed with us nearly every weekend, as her mum and Tony seemed to go away a lot together, to places that apparently weren't suitable for a fifteen-year-old. God knows why Cherry wanted to hang out at mine. My dad had only just stopped wearing flares and we didn't have any of the cool stuff Cherry had at her house, like the Soda Stream her mum and Tony had brought back last time they were away, when she'd stayed at our house for the whole two weeks.

'It's your mum's birthday next weekend, isn't it?'

'Yes, but dad always insists on going to Jimmy's, that place on the seafront that does the huge T-bone steaks, with the plastic tablecloths and a picture of the queen hanging in the window.'

'I thought the council had closed that down years ago.' Cherry wrinkled her nose.

'Dad says it's honest, and you know what you're going to get.' I raised an eyebrow. 'He doesn't seem to care that might be salmonella!'

'Leave it with me. I'll get my mum to mention to your mum how fantastic the Berni Inn is.' Cherry grinned again. 'And when you see the Andrew-lookalike, believe me, the last thing you'll be worried about is what you're having to eat!'

****

I should have known Cherry would pull it off. I think my mum was just as in awe of Cherry's mum, Julie, as I was of Cherry, so it hadn't taken much to persuade her the Berni Inn was the place for her birthday. Now here I was, in a dress from Top Shop that I'd blown all my Christmas money on, wondering if the evening could possibly live up to its promise. Planting a kiss on my favourite Wham! poster, I bid a farewell to the real Andrew and set off to find out if anyone – least of all a waiter – could really hold a candle to him.

'So what are you going to have, Janey?' Dad looked at me over the

Illustrated by **Feena Quinn**

top of his menu. I could have quoted his order without looking – prawn cocktail, steak and the chocolate fudge cake – he was so predictable. I wondered if Mum ever looked at him and thought about Julie and Tony, who still went to discos most Saturday nights; except for the times when Tony suddenly had something else to do and Julie would turn up at ours. When she did, my mum would put an arm around Julie for some reason and they'd shut themselves in the kitchen for hours, drinking Blue Nun and talking. Poor Mum, maybe she was asking Julie's advice? She must have been really envious, seeing as she spent most of her weekends curled up on the sofa with Dad watching Quincy or Columbo on the TV.

'I think I'm going to have scampi for main.' As I spoke, the waiter approached our table and I caught my breath. For once, Cherry hadn't been exaggerating. He really was the spitting image of Andrew Ridgeley. I was glad I was sitting down or my legs wouldn't have held me up.

'Ah, perfect timing!' Dad peered at the name badge pinned to Andrew's doppelganger and I knew what was going to happen. It was like watching a collision you're powerless to stop. 'So, Darren, what would you recommend?'

I contemplated sliding under the table, whilst my dad continued to talk to Darren as if he'd known him his whole life. He had this mortifying habit of reading the name badges of restaurant staff, and even shop assistants, and using their names over and over again in the ensuing conversation. If the ground had opened up at the

moment - when I'd been doing my level best to look as cool as an untrendy teenager ever could - I'd have dived right in.

I just mouthed a silent sorry to Darren instead, who smiled at me, making my stomach do a sort of funny somersault that put me right off my scampi and chips. Watching him disappear with our order, I wished I had some way of contacting Cherry to tell her she'd been right; the Andrew Ridgeley lookalike was not only here but he'd smiled at me, suggesting he understood the burden of an embarrassing dad and wouldn't hold it against me.

Desperate to check my make-up before he came back, I headed off for the toilets. And then I saw him - the Andrew-a-like - talking to a blonde waitress.

'I've got a vegetarian at my table, who keeps asking if any of the food she's ordered has been anywhere near meat!' The girl shook her head and her perfect blonde curls didn't move, whilst I wished for the millionth time my mum would let me have a perm.

'I can beat that.' Darren had his back to me as he spoke. 'I've got some wally on my table, who started calling me Daz thirty seconds after I turned up, and his teenage kid keeps staring at me with eyes like Bambi. I'm twenty-one, not fifteen and even if I was…'

****

I didn't want to hear what he was going to say next. I ran to the toilets as if my hair was on fire, never mind permed. I don't know how long I stood there, looking at myself; a stupid kid, so out of touch with the Eighties – and my own generation - that I'd never

have the sort of life someone like Cherry would. I was supposed to be marrying Andrew Ridgeley and she was going to marry John Taylor. The big difference was she actually stood a chance. By the time I'd got myself together enough to leave the toilets, my eyelashes were mascara-free and all I had to show for my make-up was an electric blue puddle in the sink.

'Janey, is that you?' Charging out of the toilets, I hit someone wearing a waiter's uniform square in the chest.

'Andy?' It was Andy Johnson, from the upper sixth, the one with the serial killer's eyebrows. Only he didn't have them anymore, he'd done something to them, and he looked good. Staring up into his smiling face, I felt it again, that sensation in my stomach that pushed all thoughts of food to one side. 'What are you doing here?'

'I got a job as a waiter on Saturday nights. It's only my second week, but I wanted to earn a bit of money of my own, so I could afford to go to the cinema and maybe even take someone with me.' He looked straight at me. 'I wondered if you wanted to come and see The Outsiders with me, next weekend? If you fancy it, maybe you can write your number down and I'll call you to set it up.'

****

'I'd like that.' I scribbled my phone number on to the order pad and I knew even then it was the start of something big. Maybe it was Andy Johnson and not an Andrew Ridgeley lookalike who'd come into my life that night. But either way Cherry was right again, the Berni Inn really could change your life!

WHICH 80's BAND ARE YOU?

1. At a gig you:
A. Head straight for the mosh pit
B. Wear earplugs unless it's an acoustic set
C. Have an Access All Areas pass
D. Volunteer to clear up the litter afterwards
E. Stand in the darkest corner

2. You are wearing:
A. An old band t-shirt and faded jeans
B. Polo shirt, chinos and a jumper draped over your shoulders
C. Leather trousers, designer t-shirt and jacket with rolled-up sleeves
D. Second-hand clothes, the baggier the better
E. Black from head to toe

3. Your hair is:
A. Long, unstyled and great for head-banging
B. Neat, tidy and trimmed every 5 weeks
C. Cut at Sassoon
D. Of little significance
E. Dyed the blackest black

4. Your drink of choice is:
A. Snakebite & Black with a Jack Daniels chaser
B. A can of Tab
C. Champagne, of course!
D. Mineral water
E. Absinthe

5. You prefer to travel:
A. On a tour bus, well stocked with alcohol
B. Not too far away from home
C. By private jet or yacht
D. As little as possible - there's my carbon footprint to consider
E. After dark and before the sun rises

6. You are married to:
A. Life on the road
B. My best friend
C. The most gorgeous person on the planet
D. Saving the Earth
E. The most perfect nightmare

7. If you won the lottery jackpot, you would:
A. Spend it on fast living
B. Use it to help my family and friends
C. Add it to my already bulging bank balance
D. Donate it to good causes
E. Buy coffins for me and my mates

8. Your favourite meal is:
A. Washed down with plenty of beer
B. Anything home-cooked
C. Eaten at The Ivy
D. Organic and Vegan
E. Garlic-free

9. You are most likely to watch:
A: Old footage of Donnington Festival
B. A romantic comedy
C. The premiere of the latest Bond film
D. A documentary on the fur trade
E. The Hammer House of Horror box set

10. The 80's song that best sums up your life is:
A. I Love Rock 'n' Roll
B. Perfect
C. Living It Up
D. World Shut Your Mouth
E. Dancing In The Dark

Results on next page >

69

WHICH 80's BAND ARE YOU?
RESULTS

Mostly A - You are Motörhead
Living life in the fast lane and listening to your music LOUD,
One thing is certain, you'd have made old Lemmy proud.

Mostly B - You are Haircut 100
Clean cut lifestyle with lots of family fun,
You're definitely one to take home to meet Mum.

Mostly C - You are Duran Duran
"Work hard, play even harder" is your motto for living.
For those close to you, you're the gift that keeps on giving.

Mostly D - You are The Smiths
A desire to put right the world is what gets you going.
You've a passion for caring, and don't mind it showing.

Mostly E - You are The Sisters of Mercy
For you, darkness and mystery are life-enhancing.
Now and then you lighten up for a bit of Goth dancing.

WHO'S THAT BOY?

Part of another trio in the Eighties, after gaining fame with a bigger band, who is stood between his two sisters in this photo?

Answer at back of book

STUCK ON YOU

There can be very few of us who grew up during the Eighties who failed to succumb to the pursuit of sticker collecting at one time or other. No matter what the theme of your collection was, there was always one elusive sticker which evaded capture. Here, 80's fan **Mark Taylor** recalls the ups and downs of the hobby, and how he came into possession of the Holy Grail of his prized collection.

"I was as skinny as a rake in the early Eighties, and I put this down to one thing mainly. While other kids asked their mums to buy them sweets and chocolate from the paper shop, and thus piled on the pounds, I asked my mum to buy me packets of stickers instead. If there was a sticker album being given away with a comic or magazine, I had to have it. Mum's contribution to the financial success of the Panini sticker company should not have been so criminally overlooked! I drove her nuts with my obsession. I tended to concentrate mostly on the popular football collections but I did also venture off into more left-field territory, such as Buck Rogers, A-Team, Fame, Return Of The Jedi, E.T. and, of course, the utterly brilliant Smash Hits Collection. However, my collecting bug didn't pass without incident.

I was the first in my class to complete the E.T. sticker album, and I took it into school to show everyone. I trotted off to lunch bursting with pride, foolishly leaving my bag unattended in the classroom with my prized album in it. When I returned for afternoon registration, I was aghast to discover that my album was gone! I went into hysterics. That album had taken me weeks to complete and had cost mum a small fortune. Instead of consoling me and calming me down, my teacher just stood there laughing at me, along with my classmates. After what seemed like an age, he pointed up towards the ceiling. I looked up to see my album stuck fast to the ceiling extractor fan, where my 'friends' had placed it, along with a note saying "TAYLOR, PHONE HOME"!

My best mate was a lad called Windy (so nicknamed because he kept 'letting one go' when he was reading aloud an extract from a book in English class). Like me, he also collected stickers and cards but always seemed to do better than me. It was the summer of '84, and a brand new shopping centre with a Texaco garage had opened near our estate. Texaco were the sponsors of that summer's One Day International cricket series, England vs West Indies. To commemorate this, they brought out a series of cards depicting caricatures of cricketers from each team. You received one every time you bought some petrol at a Texaco garage. Windy and I kept finding them in the nearby streets, fields and roadside verges, where people had just thrown them away.

There were 12 of these cards to collect. Windy bet me he would get all 12 cards before I did. Not one to shirk a challenge, I took him on. We both quickly managed to get 11 out of the 12 cards, but we both needed the same card to complete the collection: Michael Holding, the fearsome West Indies fast bowler. For the next few days, we scoured the streets in desperation, our hearts skipping a beat each time we saw the now familiar sight of an unwanted card discarded by a litter-lout motorist, only to swear profusely when it turned out to be yet another David bloody Gower! Then, one afternoon, it happened. We were playing cricket in a field nearby, and I was frustrating Windy with my dogged defensive batting. He was teasing me, saying I'd never hit a six. So, to shut him up, I DID hit him for six. The ball ended up in a stream at the far end of the field. Windy got the hump and refused to fetch the ball, so I had to go and get it. I carefully climbed down the small bank, reached across into the stream and retrieved the ball, only to go head-first into the stream. Windy was crying with laughter as I lifted myself out, soaked. I tossed him the ball

as I got back up to the top of the bank, and duly slipped and fell into some stinging nettles. Cue more hysterical laughter. I was screaming. Not from the pain of the stings, but because there, lying amongst those horrible nettles, was a Texaco Trophy Cricket Card bearing the face of Michael Holding! GET IN!! The quest was over, albeit in farcical circumstances, and poor old Windy was beaten. I ran home, feeling like Charlie Bucket did after finding Willy Wonka's last golden ticket. I couldn't wait to tell Mum and Dad, and have them lavish me with praise. Instead, all I got was "What the bloody hell have you been doing?" as I burst in through the back door, soggy, bedraggled and covered in nettle rash. Happy days!"

1987 That was the year...

Terry Waite was kidnapped

The Archbishop of Canterbury's special envoy had travelled to the Lebanon on 12th January, in the hope of securing the release of four British hostages. He was taken captive himself by Hezbollah, who believed he was spying for the CIA, on 20th January. Held in solitary confinement for more than four years, Waite was eventually released on 18th November 1991.

****

Herald of Free Enterprise capsized

Bound for Dover, the Townsend Thoresen passenger ferry began to sink shortly after leaving the Belgian port of Zeebrugge, on 6th March. The roll-on-roll-

off ferry was later found to have embarked with its bow doors still open, allowing water to enter the car deck, and causing the vessel to de-stabilise only 90 seconds after departure. The tragedy resulted in the deaths of 193 passengers and crew.

****

The Simpsons were born

The cartoon family premiered as a short animated slot on Fox network's Tracey Ullman Show on 19th April. It was later developed as a prime time show, with the first episode being broadcast on 17th December 1989.

****

Hungerford Massacre

Unemployed handyman Michael Ryan went on the rampage, armed with a handgun and two semi-automatic rifles, in the Berkshire town on 19th August. The 27-year-old fatally wounded 16 people, including his own mother, before barricading himself in his former school and shooting himself in the head.

****

Hurricane hit UK

Contrary to Michael's Fish's advice not to worry about reports of a hurricane, southern England was hit with storm force winds up to 120mph late in the evening of 15th October. Continuing through the early

hours of the following day, the storm claimed the lives of 23 people and wreaked havoc throughout the country, costing the insurance industry £2 billion.

****

Black Monday

Following the damage caused by the storm, trading was twice halted at the London Stock Exchange on 16th October. Unable to respond to declining world markets and plummeting shares in Wall Street, after a wave of panic selling in the U.S. stock market, the FTSE index crashed on 19th October, with a loss of £63 billion.

****

Lester Piggott went to jail

The retired jockey began a three year jail sentence on 23rd October, following his conviction for tax evasion.

****

King's Cross fire

Fire broke out under a wooden escalator at the London underground station as the rush hour commute was coming to an end, on 18th November.

More than 150 firefighters were sent to tackle the blaze, in which 31 people died and 100 more were injured. The cause of the fire was found to be a discarded match, leading to the banning of smoking on the underground.

****

We said a final goodbye to:

Andy Warhol, Eamonn Andrews, Fred Astaire, Fulton Mackay, Irene Handl, Lee Marvin, Liberace and Rita Hayworth.

****

UK Chart Toppers included:

Rick Astley
- Never Gonna Give You Up

T'Pau
- China In Your Hand

Bee Gees
- You Win Again

M/A/R/R/S
- Pump Up The Volume

Steve 'Silk' Hurley
- Jack Your Body

Pet Shop Boys
- It's A Sin

Mel & Kim
- Respectable

Starship
- Nothing's Gonna Stop Us Now

****

Top Films included:

Fatal Attraction, Dirty Dancing, Good Morning Vietnam, Three Men & A Baby, The Lost Boys, RoboCop, Lethal Weapon, Full Metal Jacket, Wall Street, The Living Daylights, Wish You Were Here, Mannequin, Cry Freedom, The Witches of Eastwick, and Planes, Trains and Automobiles.

****

Rear of The Year:

Anita Dobson

SECRET 80's DIARY

The Untrendy Teenager's Thoughts on...

Crushes, Discos and Discovering Boys

14th February, 1984
There was a Valentine's disco in the evening. It was good except there were too many smooches, and those of us who never get asked felt a bit left out. Got a kiss from Shaun, Joanne's boyfriend. I think she made him do it to make me feel better.

2nd March
Watched Grange Hill, it was the last one with the school disco. Stewpot and Claire are back together, and smooched at the end. That made me depressed. Why do so many people have boyfriends and not me? Also, why have they banned smelly rubbers, which I liked collecting? It's not fair.

27th March
I've got feelings for Greg again (the one I fancied in the first year). In fact I've got sexual passion for him! CENSORED! BAN!

15th June
Disco tonight. We're all gonna celebrate the end of exams and our good, and otherwise, results.

LATER: Well, we didn't really celebrate cos Mandy and that lot kept disappearing to the orgy at the back. I think I would've gone if Cathy or someone had come with me.

25th October
TOTP was good. Limahl was on, accompanied by that girl who sings with him on Never Ending Story. Lucky devil. She danced with him! I'm definitely back on him now. Mum thinks he's got little legs. He's not exactly big, but then you don't have to be big to be sexy.

30th May, 1985
Don't laugh, but I once read this book about this girl who had a crush on someone who never noticed her, whilst someone else loved her. Would you believe that's my position? Thought not, but someone actually FANCIES me! And guess who? It's Ralf! [met on current school trip to Germany].

31st May
The next thing I knew I was French kissing him, and although I nearly choked on his tongue, it wasn't half as bad as I'd thought! I thought, "Wow, I can kiss!" Then I did choke and we both cracked up. Ralf said, "Even when you do this you are funny!" We kissed several times after that, and I remember Simple Minds' 'Don't You Forget About Me' playing in the background.

5th June
Asked Dad if I could go back to Germany in the summer, but he said we couldn't afford it. I can understand that and I don't blame them at all, but I'm so upset cos it means I can't see Ralf until next

year! My first boyfriend, and he has to be 6 billion miles away! I must buy some heart notepaper to write to him on, and get him something lovey-dovey for his birthday, which is in July. Started my Germany project for school, which is a bit like a diary with drawings and diagrams. It will have to be edited though. I don't think my parents and teachers will appreciate pearls of wisdom such as "I got my first snog to Simple Minds". Got very tired and depressed at tea, and started crying later on the phone to Ros, so I got shouted at. They just don't care. I suppose they've never had a boyfriend 500 or so miles away. Or girlfriend in Dad's case.

20th June
NEWS OF THE DAY: I got a phone call from RALF! All the way from Germany! And he said it was boring there without me. I said I missed him and oh, I felt like those girls on TV whose boyfriends rang up!

4th August
Spent the day listening to Germany songs. I miss it so much, especially Ralf. I BLOODY WELL WANT TO KISS HIM, and usually end up kissing Lenny the toy lion instead. Mind you, that won't really do because if I kissed Lenny like I kissed Ralf I would get a mouthful of fluff. So I peck him only. Sorry to go on about snogging, but it's still a novelty to me and it's very frustrating that now I've found a boy who is actually willing to do it, it is impossible. Mind you, I nearly choked several times on his tongue. He put me straight onto French kissing without even asking! I am now wondering how you keep your tongue out of the way on a simple English snog.

20th July
On Brookside, Damon picked up this girl. Five months ago I'd have been jealous as hell, but not now. Maybe it's because I've finally got a boyfriend (of sorts) of my own. It's stupid having crushes on people. No, I like having crushes on them, but you're never going to go out with them. I've only started thinking like this since Ralf. Mind you, I am still enjoying my current crushes on Boris Becker and Rik Mayall. Boris has got a 17 year old girlfriend. Silly cow! Still, I've got Ralf I suppose, and Boris is only a fantasy.

11th August
A really sad letter from Ralf. He said what I've been thinking for ages, that it would be better if we were just good friends. It was really hard for him to write it. He said I could have my boyfriend in England if I wanted. Greg maybe?! I'm not really that upset – it couldn't last.

15th October
We saw a video of the German exchange. RALF in full colour and life! I was creasing up while it was on, but for the rest of the day I felt like crying. Tonight I have been playing Germany songs again.

29th October
This week seems to be going so slowly. Today, we got German and Maths, and I can't do it. I will go MAD soon! I'm firmly convinced that I will hate school for ever. We have got six weeks of it at least before Christmas. I am feverishly trying not to compare it with last year or it gets unbearable. I keep getting spots and my hair keeps going greasy.

I AM DEPRESSED, DEPRESSED, DEPRESSED! I usually play Germany tapes and escape into Germany with Ralf, seeing as Greg clearly finds me repulsive, but I am considering a nervous breakdown.

3rd November
Greg was back today. I kept staring at him in assembly. God, why is he so sexy when he's so horrible?

6th November
Now the Thatcher government have done it. They have taken away the only decent radio station [Laser 558] in the whole world. I HATE THEM! I can safely say that nobody has ever brought me as much pleasure as Charlie did. I'm now resigned to never hearing him again, but I know I'll never forget him, or Laser. It's been an important chapter in my life. Goodbye, Charlie darling. Thanks for all you did.

9th November
Today I have felt better in body, but completely screwed up in mind. It will be all Charlie's fault if I fail my O levels. I can't bear that I'll never hear him again. He's like a drug. He is NOT an ordinary crush.

23rd November
The frantic babbling about Ralf and Greg took its toll and I had very weird dreams. Firstly one about Ralf in Germany next year, when we were trying really hard to be good friends. Woke up at 5.00am, felt sad, went back to sleep and dreamed about Greg. But I'd much rather love Ralf than Greg, as he wouldn't hurt me and Greg would.

29th November
I got to sleep a little earlier, after thinking a lot. I'd come to the conclusion that I was only hanging onto Ralf for the sake of it because I haven't got another boyfriend. If I could only go out with someone I'd let him go, but English boys are so pig-headed and only go for looks (well, mainly). I decided that I couldn't go out with him again and mustn't hope to, although I still think a lot about him.

That Was Then, But This Is Now

As the popularity of 80's music continues to grow, so does the demand for the decade's top artists both within and outside of the retro music circuit.

Juggling the job of fronting Spandau Ballet, solo appearances, a Saturday night DJ slot on Absolute 80s, and even a stint in the jungle at the end of last year, Tony Hadley typifies the 80's star whose light is still burning bright.

Following in the frontman's footsteps in radio presenting, fellow band member Martin Kemp teamed up with Fearne Cotton during the summer, to co-host Graham Norton's Saturday morning Radio 2 show, further illustrating 80's artists' diversification throughout the music and entertainment industries.

An 80's icon who took his DJ set to live audiences in 2016, ahead of The Specials' autumn tour, is Terry Hall.

Playing an eclectic mix of tracks including Janet Kay's 'Silly Games' and Deee-lite's 'Groove Is In The Heart' when he visited Whitstable, the Two-Tone pioneer rose to even greater heights in my already stratospheric opinion of him as he

Terry Hall

segued Prince Buster's 'Al Capone' into Ini Kamoze's 'Here Comes The Hot Stepper'. Not the most obvious pairing but it worked, and then some.

Another unlikely combination this year was the teaming up of Midge Ure, Jazzie B and Peter Hook in the search to find the UK's Best Part-Time Band. Hosted by Rhod Gilbert, the BBC 4 four part series saw each of the musicians pick their two favourite part-time bands, who then competed in the final show. Not only did the programme reveal the vast wealth of undiscovered

Jazzie B

talent within Britain, but gave an insight into the musical breadth of the three competing musicians who, since the Eighties, have each become synonymous with a particular music genre.

Ian Donaldson

One artist who has pushed the boundaries of his 80's pigeonholing is Ian Donaldson.

Making a welcome return to recording after a break of almost thirty years, the former H2O frontman released his first solo single from the forthcoming album 'And Then We Take The Stars' this autumn. The debut track 'Angel Pale' describes how the singer's life was transformed after watching David Bowie perform 'Star Man' on Top of The Pops - "My life began in Ziggy's reign" - and was written some 18 months before we lost the legendary performer at the beginning of the year.

Featuring background glimpses of glam rock and Ziggy-style guitar, there is no doubting the song's influences.

Adam Ant

Yet, the feel good vibe to this coming-of-age tribute is undeniable and will have you singing along by the second play.

Equally catchy and guaranteed to have you bopping around, is 'Twenty Something' by The Pet Shop Boys, the second single from their album 'Super' released in April.

Entering the charts at Number 3, the pop pair's offering is their 16th album to make the UK Top Ten. With such enduring popularity, the stalwarts of synth embarked upon the album's tour in October, and will be playing UK dates next February.

Also continuing to release new material in a style that is unmistakably theirs, but at the same time contemporary, are Deacon Blue and ABC. Ricky Ross and Co. released the title track off the album 'The Believers' in August, immediately followed by a tour.

Further illustrating the purchasing power of 40-somethings, ABC's release of 'Lexicon of Love II' in June saw the album enter the charts at Number 5. Including the tracks 'Viva Love' and 'The Flames of Desire', the album was performed in its entirety during the band's UK tour which began in October, and included The Royal Festival Hall amongst the venues played.

A classic 80's album played live in its entirety in 2016 was 'Kings of The Wild Frontier' during Adam Ant's spring tour.

In addition to the Burundi Beat-based album, Mr. Goddard performed some of his solo tracks including 'Goody Two Shoes' and 'Vive Le Rock', as well as early Adam & The Ants tracks such as 'Zerox', 'Never Trust A Man (With Egg on His Face)' and 'Cartrouble'.

The result was a joyous two hours from the inimitable Dandy Highwayman.

Still to play in the UK, Culture Club embarked on their tour of the U.S.A. in July.

Performing a set that included most of the tracks on their 'Colour By Numbers' album and hits such as Karma Chameleon and Victims, the band delighted audiences across the States. Fingers crossed they choose to do so in the UK at some point in the near future. Even a one-off gig like the one Duran Duran did at The Eden Project in June would be much appreciated by us fans.

In contrast, one of the most prolific performers on the 80's retro circuit, and with a Number 1 album this year under his belt, is Rick Astley.

Entering the UK charts at Number 1 shortly after its release in June, his 2016 album '50', which includes the singles 'Dance' and 'Angels On My Side', stayed inside the Top 10 for a further seven consecutive weeks.

It was the Newton-le-Willows singer's first time at the top of the album charts since 1987, when he accomplished the same feat with 'Whenever You Need Somebody'. Here's hoping Rick's success heralds the return of 80's artists back at the top, where they belong.

Rick Astley

COMING ON STRONG WITH
JAMIE MOSES

The name Jamie Moses may not be familiar, yet I can guarantee you will have heard him play.

The Anglo-American rock guitarist has literally worked with an A to Z of artists, from Anastacia to Zucchero, including Gary Barlow, U2, Pete Townshend, Chaka Khan, Beyoncé and Freddie Mercury. Regularly touring with Sir Tom Jones, Jamie has been second guitarist for Queen since 1992, and counts Brian May as a close friend: "Brian has been so good to me over the years, and it's nice to talk guitars with Brian because we identify with each other … and he's one of my heroes, so that helps as well."

Despite his association with Rock and Pop royalty, it is his involvement with 80's band Broken English, which also featured founder lead singer Steve Elson and guitarist Alan Coates, we first discuss.

It was through Alan that Jamie got his place in the trio, having been introduced some years previously:

"We knew each other since the late Seventies, when I used to go and see a band that he played with called Sprinkler. Then Alan joined The Hollies. He was with them doing all of Graham Nash's bits … and in 1984, I ended up filling in for him on an Australian tour."

Broken English formed in 1987, and it was their first single 'Comin' On Strong', released in May that year, which became their biggest success. Peaking at Number 18, the track spent 11 weeks in the UK charts, due in no small part to the fact that it sounded remarkably like a Rolling Stones track.

"'Comin' On Strong' was a little trick that we did," admits Jamie. "After we recorded it, they sent it out on a white label … to all the radio stations … with no information at all on it. [The radio stations] put it on and went "Fuck me, it's the Stones! This must be their new single." So, everybody started playing it, assuming it was the Stones. That's largely why it was successful, I think, because of that. It was a good little ploy."

I joke that it certainly wasn't due to the song's video, which features the band performing sequenced dancing, whilst dressed in outfits that make them look like a cross between soldiers of fortune and the Ghostbusters.

"Well, the next one was slightly less embarrassing, but not much," Jamie replies.

That second video was for "Love on The Side", a single which had a track written by the brother of Bruno Brookes on the B-side. It was rumoured that once the powers-that-be at Radio 1 found this out, the track disappeared from their playlist. I ask Jamie if there is any truth in that rumour.

"Well, I'll never know because the management of that band, which included Steve [Elson] kept everything so close to their chests. Myself and Alan were informed of

very little that went on. It wasn't until the band split up that we realised that when EMI wanted to renew our contract, they [the management] went in to the offices without any discussion with us and asked for a quarter of a million pounds, or something ridiculous, and EMI just laughed them out of the building.

Rather than tell Jamie and Alan exactly what had happened, the pair were simply told "Oh, EMI didn't renew your contract, boys … bad news, sorry about that." So, the band decided to split up.

In stark contrast, Los Pacaminos, the Tex-Mex band Jamie co-founded with Paul Young in 1992, has stood the test of time. With the band celebrating its 25th anniversary next year, I ask if there are any plans in the pipeline to mark the occasion.

"We reckon more of us will be dead by then, so we don't know really," answers Jamie. He is referring to the recent passing of Matt Irving, the band's keyboard and accordion player. The talented and much missed musician, who played bass guitar for Manfred Mann's Earth Band from 1981 to 1986, passed away in 2015 after battling prostate cancer, much to the devastation of the band and its fans.

"The band's the same as it's always been, except with the very sad loss of Matt Irving," says Jamie. "I love it. As much as anything with that band, it's like the Pacaminos' social club. We've been friends for 25 years, most of us. It's just really great to see the guys, and when we actually have a string of dates and we go on a small tour, it's the best thing in the world … and then coming home to the family is the best thing in the world."

Anyone who has seen Los Pacaminos perform will agree the camaraderie amongst the musicians, an accomplished bunch which includes Drew Barfield, Melvin Duffy, Steve Greetham, Mark Pinder and Jim Russell, is undeniable. That friendship has been known to extend to guest Pacaminos appearances by old mates Bob Geldof and Average White Band's Hamish Stuart.

Add to that, the band welcoming the audience into its fold, not only with cheeky little numbers like 'Mi Chorizo' but with regular tequila breaks, during which ladies are invited to bring the Pacs shots of tequila, is it any wonder everyone leaves feeling happy and, dare I say, ever so slightly inebriated?

"It's a no pressure gig, the Pacaminos," explains Jamie. "It plays itself. The whole idea is to go on stage and have fun. That's the whole concept of the band … and it's not contrived. It's not fucking One Direction, you know. It was put together with the aim of having fun, as a side project for all of us, and it's slowly turning into more than that.

It's only taken 24 years!" he laughs.

Jamie Moses and Paul Young

Los Pacaminos - L-R Hamish Stuart, Drew Barfield, Paul Young, Matt Irving, Jamie Moses, Steve Greetham

Matthew Rudd's
Top 10 One Hit Wonders

Host of Absolute 80s' Sunday night radio show Forgotten 80s, Matthew Rudd is no stranger to delving into the depths of the Eighties' charts, in search of the decade's underplayed gems. Some of the greatest tracks he uncovers were recorded by artists who only once managed to feature in the UK Top 40. With the Eighties boasting a wealth of these One Hit Wonders to choose from, Matthew picks his ten favourites.

****

Twilight Café
- Susan Fassbender

"A slick, dark and yet joyful bit of retro pop. The unusual name and unshowbizzy image of the lady in question made it all the more compelling."
Co-written with Fassbender's song writing partner Kay Russell, 'Twilight Café' spent 6 weeks in the UK Top 40 in 1981, peaking at Number 21. Their subsequent releases 'Stay' (released as Fassbender-Russell) and 'Merry-Go-Round' failed to chart, resulting in the pair being dropped by CBS Records.

****

The First Picture of You -
The Lotus Eaters

"Slowburning intro, heartfelt vocals, big drum intro into one of the best choruses of the decade."
Liverpool band The Lotus Eaters

encapsulated the Summer of '83, spending a total of 12 weeks in the UK charts with 'The First Picture of You'. Reaching its highest position of Number 15 in August, the track was the band's only Top 40 entry, although their follow-up single 'You Don't Need Someone New' did hit Number 53.

****

Big In Japan - Alphaville

"Icy electronic noise and lyrical dexterity epitomising the mid-decade, rising above some of the Europop dirges and becoming a bonafide pop anthem."
During a 14 week chart run in 1984, including three weeks in the Top 10, 'Big In Japan' was the only single from German band Alphaville to make the UK Top 40. Despite their next release 'Forever Young' being a Top 20 hit across Europe, and topping the charts in Sweden, the track only made it as far as Number 98 in the UK charts.

****

Waiting For A Train
- Flash and The Pan

"It just makes you move!"
Charting high in their native Australia during the late Seventies, Flash and The Pan achieved one-off chart success in the UK in 1983, with 'Waiting For A Train'. Achieving its top spot of Number 7, during a nine week run in the UK Top 40, the single was followed up by 'Down Among The Dead Men', which attained Number 77 as its highest chart position.

****

Tantalise (Wo Wo Ee Yeh Yeh) - Jimmy The Hoover

"Understated jungle drum ditty with a simple but tuneful 'woah yeah yeah" chorus that stayed with you for ages."
Produced by Steve Levine, 'Tantalise' spent six weeks in the UK Top 40 during the Summer of '83. Fronted by singer Derek Dunbar, and managed by Malcolm McLaren, Jimmy The Hoover released their follow-up single 'Kill Me Kwik' later that year. Despite having the benefit of being produced by the Art of Noise's Ann Dudley, the track failed to enter the charts.

****

Broken Land
- The Adventures

"Big-deal, piano-heavy rock anthem bemoaning the troubles in Northern Ireland while showing off a genuinely high level of musicianship."
Northern Irish band The Adventures had seven singles enter the UK charts (Top 100) during the Eighties, but 'Broken Land' was their only release to make it to the UK Top 40. Peaking at Number 20, the song spent 12 weeks in the UK charts in 1988, five of which were in the Top 40.

****

Since Yesterday -
Strawberry Switchblade

"Classical samples, synthetic rhythms, sweetheart vocals and polka dots. What's not to like?"
Comprised of Jill Bryson and Rose

McDowell, Strawberry Switchblade enjoyed a 20 week run in the UK charts, from October 1984, with 'Since Yesterday'. Peaking at Number 5, the single was followed by a handful of releases, including a cover of Dolly Parton's Jolene, none of which entered the UK Top 40.

****

I Beg Your Pardon
- Kon Kan

"The most underrated sampler record of all. Original lyrics put on top of bits swiped from Spagna, Silver Convention and Lynn Anderson. Innovative and respectful and never done for the sake of it."

First charting in March 1989, 'I Beg Your Pardon' achieved 13 weeks in the UK charts, including two consecutive weeks at its highest position of Number 5. Kon Kan's subsequent release 'Harry Houdini' would reach no higher than Number 88.

****

Let My People Go-Go
- The Rainmakers

"A slice of alternative American blue collar rawk with an infectious bridge and chorus."
Peaking at Number 18, 'Let My People Go-Go' spent six weeks in the UK Top 40 during the spring of 1987. Although The Rainmakers released three (non-charting)

studio albums during the Eighties, none of the albums produced a follow-up single in the UK.

****

A Walk In The Park
- Nick Straker Band

"Where the disco and the new wave that breasted the 70s and 80s met, and a terrific pop sound was made."
Beginning its 12 week chart run in August 1980, 'A Walk In The Park' spent three consecutive weeks at Number 20, its highest position. Nick Straker Band's subsequent release 'Leaving on The Midnight Train' attained no higher than Number 61 in the UK charts.

80's Chart Toppers
With (jingle) bells on!

There is only one thing better than having a Number 1 single, and that is taking the top spot at Christmas. In the days when X-Factor domination of the festive season was merely a glint in Simon Cowell's eye, this is what the Eighties gave us for Christmas chart toppers.

****

1980
St Winifred's School Choir - There's No One Quite Like Grandma
Smacking of sentimentality, the saccharine sweet tune spent two weeks in the top spot, having superceded John Lennon's (Just Like) Startin' Over in the prime position. He later ousted the Stockport children's choir on 10th January 1981, with Imagine.

****

1981
Human League - Don't You Want Me
Despite a heavy chart presence during the first half of the decade, this was the band's only Number 1 single, spending five weeks at the top of the chart and a further 8 weeks inside the Top 40.

1982
Renée & Renato - Save Your Love
Having entered the charts at the end of October, the slushy duet made it to the top a week before Christmas, and stayed there for four weeks. It replaced Beat Surrender, the final single recorded by The Jam, and the band's last Number 1.

****

1983
Flying Pickets - Only You
The former Yazoo hit saw the A Cappella band put an end to the five week run of success of Billy

Joel's Uptown Girl, replacing it with their own five weeks of chart leadership.

****

1984
Band Aid
- Do They Know It's Christmas
The charity single, recorded to raise funds for Ethiopian famine relief, entered the charts at Number 1 on 15th December. It stayed there for five weeks until 19th January 1985, when it was toppled by Foreigner's I Want To Know What Love Is.

****

1985
Shakin' Stevens - Merry Christmas Everyone
The Welsh rocker scored his fourth Number 1 with this festive track. Spending two weeks in the top slot, the single spent a further six weeks inside the Top 40 upon its initial release.

A Christmas favourite, it continues to enjoy flirtations with the chart periodically.

****

1986
Jackie Wilson
- Reet Petite
Originally released in 1957, the track went on to spend four weeks at the top of the chart 29 years later. The song was accompanied by a clay animation video, first seen on BBC's Arena documentary series.

****

1987
Pet Shop Boys - Always On My Mind
Beating The Pogues and Kirsty MacColl's Fairytale of New York to the Christmas top ranking, the former Elvis hit was the third of four Number Ones for the duo. Topping the chart for four weeks, it was replaced by Belinda Carlisle's Heaven Is A Place On Earth, on 16th January 1988.

****

1988
Cliff Richard
- Mistletoe & Wine
Seemingly synonymous with Christmas, and with 14 Number Ones to his credit, this was the first of only two solo festive chart toppers for Cliff. Spending four weeks riding high, his 80's seasonal success exceeded that of any other decade, with 1990's Saviour's Day only managing to hold onto its peak place for one week.

****

1989
Band Aid II
- Do They Know It's Christmas
Fittingly finishing a decade of change and transformation this re-recording, produced by Stock Aitken and Waterman, spent three weeks in pole position and continued the fundraising legacy of its predecessor five years earlier.

1988 That was the year...

The Iron Lady set a record

Having been in power for 8 years and 244 days, Margaret Thatcher became the UK's longest serving Prime Minister of the 20th century, on 3rd January. She continued to hold the position until 28th November 1990, when she formally tendered her resignation to the Queen, and left Downing Street for the final time.

****

Red Nose Day launched

Held on 5th February, the first Red Nose Day raised £15 million for Comic Relief.

****

Channel Tunnel

Simultaneous tunnelling and construction commenced in Folkestone, Kent and Coquelles, France on 28th February. The tunnel ends met on 1st December 1990, and the completed project was officially opened on 6th May 1994.

****

SLDP Formed

Founded in 1859, the Liberal Party came to an end on 3rd March, when it merged with the SDP to form the Social and Liberal Democratic Party (SLDP).

****

GCSEs were introduced

The first General Certificate of Secondary Education exams were taken by 16-year-old pupils, when the summer testing period commenced in May. Replacing the O-Level and CSE qualifications, the new awards graded coursework, undertaken over a two year period, in addition to a final exam.

****

Gazza went to White Hart Lane

Paul Gascoigne left Newcastle United and signed for Tottenham Hotspur on 18th July. The 21-year-old midfielder's move cost £2.2 million, a record-breaking transfer fee in British football. That record was broken shortly afterwards on 2nd August, when Everton paid £2.3 million for West Ham striker Tony Cottee.

****

Seoul hosted the Olympic Games

Running between 17th September and 2nd October in the South Korean capital, it was only the second time in the Games' history that the event had been held in Asia.

****

Clapham Junction disaster

On 12th December, a signal failure led to a three train collision south of London's Clapham Junction station. The crash resulted in 35 deaths and over 400 injuries.

****

Lockerbie bombing

Bound for New York's JFK Airport, Pan Am flight 103 exploded over the Scottish town on 21st December. The attack by Libyan terrorists killed all 243 passengers and 16 crew on board, and claimed 11 further victims on the ground.

****

We said a final goodbye to:

Andy Gibb, Charles Hawtrey, Divine, Kenneth Williams, Roy Kinnear, Roy Orbison, Russell Harty and Sylvester.

****

UK Chart Toppers included:

Yazz & The Plastic Population
- The Only Way Is Up

Tiffany
- I Think We're Alone Now

Bros
- I Owe You Nothing

Robin Beck
- First Time

S'Express
- Theme From S'Express

Kylie Minogue
- I Should Be So Lucky

Glenn Medeiros
- Nothing's Gonna Change My
Love For You.

****

Top Films included:

Die Hard,
Rain Man,
Buster,
A Fish Called Wanda,
Coming To America,
The Accused,
Young Guns,
Dangerous Liaisons,
Big, Working Girl,
Beetlejuice,
The Last Temptation of Christ,
Willow,
and Who Framed Roger Rabbit?

****

Rear of The Year:
Su Pollard

20 Questions
with Modern Romance's
Andy Kyriacou

Andy Kyriacou joined Modern Romance in 1981, and was the band's drummer until it split in 1985. Having reformed the band in 2001, with a brand new line-up, and Andy now on lead vocals, Modern Romance continue to tour, performing classic hits such as "Best Years of Our Lives", "Ay Ay Ay Ay Moosey" and "Everybody Salsa".

****

1. What is your favourite 80's song?

Oh my God, talk about starting with one of the most difficult questions ever! This is like asking me to tell you which blade of grass I like best in the local park. However, it is no secret that one of my favourite ever songs from the 80's, and which I consider to be a perfect pop song, was The Reflex by Duran Duran - one of the best pop bands ever.

****

2. What was the best 80's TV programme?

I didn't actually watch too much TV in the 80's. I was too busy touring the world with some band called Modern Romance. I did watch the usual stuff when I was home – Kenny Everett Show, Cheers, Miami Vice, Mork & Mindy, Minder.

****

3. Who was your teenage crush?

First it was Alexandra Bastedo, then later, Deborah Shelton. When I joined Modern Romance, I thought Kim Wilde was hot, so meeting her backstage at the Royal Variety Show, I just found my feet nailed to the floor!

****

4. What was your favourite subject at school?

My favourite subject was English, and I wasn't too bad at it. I recall we were once given the beginning of a sentence with which to create a fictional story. I was given: "The clock struck three" and I managed to turn it into a story about a serial killer who tortured his victims before actually killing them, and recorded their screams so he could listen later. I remember my teacher's written comment was: "Excellent punctuation and grammar. Vivid imagination!"

****

5. What job would you have done if you hadn't been a drummer?

I would have probably worked in an office somewhere. I actually worked in banking for 3 years when I first left school. Imagine … people entrusting ME with their money - it's a mad world!!! I am a tidy freak and have a home filing system like no other, so an office environment would probably have been my thing.

****

6. What do you miss most about the Eighties?

The nightlife. Going out to clubs, and getting in as a VIP guest was fantastic. I was an honorary member at Stringfellow's, The Hippodrome, The Blitz, Hombres, Xenon, Crackers, Bootleggers, the lot - plus I could take guests with me. In fact, I recall getting 20 guests into Stringfellow's one night – and I wasn't even there!!! All done via the phone. The fun didn't end at the clubs. Even the restaurants we went to in the early hours after the clubs would close, were full of celebs and characters.

****

7. What was the first single you ever bought?

Gentle On My Mind by Dean Martin. And I still have it.

****

8. Where did you perform your first gig?

In my bedroom. It was, of course, an imaginary gig which occurred nightly as I taught myself to play drums. My first "gig" was repeated nightly, as I tried to learn all the tracks on the Ziggy Stardust & The Spiders From Mars album, imagining I was with a band playing in front of a live crowd. I may have even stood up and taken a bow at the end! In my defence, I was only 14 or 15. As my drumming stamina and technique improved, I began "gigging" with Status Quo and then the Average White Band. Then it was Deep Purple, Earth Wind & Fire, and others. I toured the world with numerous bands, and all from my bedroom!

My first real gig was in Islington Town Hall, with a band called Kreole (named after the Elvis film King Creole). My friend still has a blurry video recording of it, originally made using one of the first portable cine cameras. Our performance is pretty awful from a presentation point of view – no discipline, no structure, but it was great fun.

Photo credit:
Harriet Armstrong Photography

9. Where is the best place you have ever visited?

Well, I have to say New York, only because I think that in a previous life I must have been a New Yorker. How else do you explain the feeling that "I am home" every time I go there?

10. Which five people, living or dead, would be your ideal dinner guests?

Imagine this lot in a room together – fun, laughter, GREAT singing – all the stuff which keeps us all young(ish): Elvis, Oscar Wilde, Marvin Gaye, Barry Humphries as Dame Edna Everage, and Sacha Baron Cohen as Borat.

11. Who is the most famous person you have ever met?

Oh Lordy! Another "needle in a haystack" question. Remember, I was on TOTP with the likes of Wham!, Culture Club, Duran, etc. so I met them all in some capacity. I still have pics of me with a few of them. However, one guy who I had a one-on-one conversation with for over an hour in 1984, and who was really charming and normal, was Freddie Mercury. What a lovely guy.

12. Which pet hate would you consign to Room 101?

Religion. Imagine if we could erase religion throughout the world, simply by waving a magic wand or indeed, disposing of it in Room 101. The result? Thousands of lives saved every day. Moneywise, millions immediately saved in warfare and spent instead, on helping people, building infrastructure, etc.

13. What makes you angry?

Most of the "phobias" & "isms" in this world. Homophobia, xenophobia, racism, sexism.

14. What is the last book you read?

The Curious Incident of The Dog In The Night-Time. An excellent read.

Although, I was rather disappointed when I saw the theatre production. The book was so much better.

15. What are you most proud of?

My two daughters, Steph and Nats, and the way they have turned out. They are both intelligent, with a good command of the English language - not easy in today's world of texting. They have a great sense of humour (sometimes a warped sense of humour like their dad – I love it), are both very humble and not at all expectant or greedy. They possess a great sense of irony, are extremely polite and appreciative of all they receive, and equally important as all of the above, they share a genuine love and fondness for each other which is so very rare in siblings. Yes, I am very proud.

16. What would be your perfect day?

Arsenal to beat Spurs at their crappy White Hart Lane ground on the last day of the season, resulting in Arsenal winning the Premier League, and as a result of that same match, Spurs being relegated, after which I go on to a Modern Romance gig at Wembley. Following that, out for a Chinese or Greek meal, where I have to act as

peacemaker between three women who all want to take me home with them, and in the end, the only logical conclusion is reached – I take all three of them back home with me …

17. What is the best Christmas present you've ever had?

Having Steph and Nats with me for the first time on a Christmas day, after separating with their mother. I will never forget the special feeling I had that day – just us three, a real fireplace, and watching them delve into their stockings before opening their main presents.

18. And the worst?

The following Christmas day - without them, as it was her turn that year.

19. What do you want for Christmas this year?

A hit record.

20. What are your hopes for the future?

To watch my two little girls do well in life, and both be happy, whilst their dad continues to make music and in doing so, earns money to look after their needs. Everything else is a bonus.

EVERYTHING 80s CROSSWORD

ACROSS

2 Kevin Bacon's character in Footloose (3,9)

8 1981 FA Cup winners, in short (5)

10 Brazilian Formula One racing driver initially (1,1)

12 37 down was one of these (3)

13 Were we fixated with this Calvin Klein perfume? (9)

16 Culture Club's backing singer initially had a solo Top 40 hit in 1984 (1,1)

17 This aftershave, launched in 1988, came in a distinctive black & white bottle (4)

19 Grifter, Strika and Boxers (5)

20 Was Emilio Estevez the Man in this 1984 film? (4)

21 Initially Sesame Street's comedy duo (1,1,1)

22 **and 39 across** Ms Joyner in brief had infamous nails (3,2)

23 Absolute 80s DJ Christian O'Connell in short (1,1)

25 Terence Trent D'Arby had a wishing one in 1987 (4)

26 Initially the nickname of Great Britain's 1988 ski jumper (1,1,1)

29 and 33 across, 37 across Start of Bananarama's 1987 First Degree hit (4,2,3)

31 Initially he composed the 1986 soundtrack to The Mission (1,1)

33 See 29 across

35 Fashion antennae (5,7)

37 See 29 across

38 Initially this 1984 film wasn't a good bet (1,1,1)

39 See 22 across

40 Popping candy (5,4)

42 Quantum Leap's Beckett (3)

44 Spin-off series featuring 56 across (1,1,1,1,4)

46 Jon was Garfield's (5)

49 Homer Simpson's trademark exclamation (3)

50 She played Pearl in Starlight Express initially (1,1)

51 ___ Communications released Doctorin' The Tardis (1,1,1)

54 Initially the brand behind 17 across (1,1,1)

56 Jill Gascoigne's character in The Gentle Touch (6,6)

60 The SDP's David (4)

62 Press Gang's Spike Thomson actor initially (1,1)

63 Initially the character played by Erica Gimpel in Fame (1,1)

64 Mike Read had one on Saturdays (10)

DOWN

1 Blockbusters had a hot one (4)

2 Initially this bunny was framed in 1988 (1,1)

3 New York was where Kurt Russell did this in the 1981 film (6)

4 **and 52 down** Foot in the 1989 Daniel Day Lewis film (2,4)

5 Veggie doll craze of 1983 (7,5,4)

6 Midfielder for 8 across in short had a dream (5)

7 Apollonia Kotero was one for Prince (4)

8 The place for awkward dancing and sneaky snogging? (6,5)

9 It was the only way for Yazz in 1988 (2)

11 Nik Kershaw's neckwear (5)

14 Motorcycling stuntman initially (1,1)

15 Initially the late singer with Visage (1,1)

17 Gem in the sequel to Romancing The Stone (5)

18 Barefoot female runner (4,4)

24 Ovett's rival, Sebastian (3)

27 Saturday morning chaos presented by Chris Tarrant and Sally James (6)

28 ___ Vogue recorded Hold On in 1989 (2)

30 Luka's Suzanne (4)

32 Snooker's Tony was The Cat (3)

34 Nick or Zandra (6)

36 Wham!'s girls initially (1,1,1)

37 William Shatner's Hooker (1,1)

41 Equipment for 32 down (3)

42 Little Fingers or Records (5)

43 Harry did it with Sally (3)

45 Icy puppies? (5)

47 River where 17 down could be found (4)

48 Malibu is a white one (3)

49 EastEnders' Roly or Willy (3)

52 See 4 down

53 Trucker's radio communication (1,1)

54 Times by two for playground toy (2)

55 Initially care should be taken handling this Bon Jovi album (1,1,1)

57 Turn it up to 11! (3)

58 ___ Dawn Chong, actress in Soul Man and The Color Purple (3)

59 "Flippin' ___, Tucker!" was uttered many times by Grange Hill's Benny Green (3)

61 They couldn't wait initially in 1986 (1,1)

The Untrendy Teenager's Thoughts on...

Smash Hits, Shopping & Fashion

28th January, 1984
Went up town. Bought (well, Mum did) a donkey jacket and pixie boots. They will make me look really trendy! About time. Maybe someone will fancy me now.

9th February
The latest fashions are pastel coloured things – bags, clothes, jewellery, etc. They are gorgeous and I'm now saving birthday money like mad for a pair of dungarees. Started my collection off well though. For my birthday, Jenny bought me a set consisting of three bangles and a necklace in pastel blue. Then I bought some sleeper earrings in pastel pink, but I can't put them in and nor can anyone else. Then I opened Cathy's present which is great. It's a little basket in pastel pink which, according to Cathy, is the height of fashion, plus a pair of pastel pink earrings. Doing well, huh?

19th March
There was a brill stall down the market with lots of Duran stuff. It was ace! I bought a Duran scarf and hat, a sew-on patch, a poster (for 20p) and two badges. Then the chap on the stall let me have a free badge as I'd spent so much! Found a gorgeous pastel blue flying suit for only £10.50,

which is now resident chez moi.

25th May
Tiffany had one of those fab new Duran bags. It's not fair. She's only just converted, and still has a Boy George lamp, cushion and scarf.

7th July
We went to the seaside and went round the market. We didn't have any money (I'm £10 in debt) so we're going back tomorrow. Ros wants a Duran t-shirt and I want a Frankie one and a bracelet to match a snazzy necklace I bought this morning. Everything's much cheaper there, e.g. a white bangle was 99p in Etam but 35p there!

21st July
Smash Hits said that Alison Moyet's 'Love Resurrection' was rude. Now they mention it, the line 'but a warm injection is all I need' is a bit, er, suggestive. That Pointer Sisters one (Jump For My Love) isn't all that moral either. I suppose Mike Read daren't open his mouth again.

25th July
There was a fab T-shirt stall at the show with badges and heart shaped cushions. I looked for one with Roger on, but the only member of Duran I could see was John. There were

loads of Duran badges. I nearly bought one saying I heart Roger but it wasn't a very good pic.

3rd August
Simon Le Bon is on the front cover of Smash Hits. I had a sneaky look through and discovered that Divine is a MAN!!!! In The Sun, it says that he eats lots of eggs and bacon for breakfast, about three salads for lunch with Coke, and rather a lot for dinner including a family size bowl of Birds' Trifle.

15th September
Bought the 12" of Agadoo for £2.35. It's ACE! So is the B-side, on which there is an X-rated version of Superman. I can see why! It says things like "1-2-3-4, give 'em a flash!" and "Show us your boobs!" and instead of Superman it says "Supercock!" But there's a chicken on afterwards so perhaps they mean that sort of cock.

19th October
Played my tapes tonight and sorted through some clothes. Experimented with some make-up to make myself beautiful, cos I'm sick of not being asked out cos I wear glasses. Part of a beauty poster from Jackie was helpful for this.

19th December

The Smash Hits Readers' Poll is fab. Duran have won Best Group, Simon Best Male Singer, John most Fanciable Male, Wild Boys Best Single and Video, Seven and The Ragged Tiger Best LP. Frankie have come 3rd in Best Group, 4th and 6th in Best Video with Two Tribes and Relax. Holly has come 9th in Best Male Singer and 4th in Most Fanciable Male (in which Roger came 7th, Mac McCulloch 20th and Mark O'Toole 8th) and also 3rd in Most Promising Act. Oh, and Relax is No. 5 in Best Single, Two Tribes No. 3, and Pleasure Dome is No. 5 in Best Album. The Young Ones has won Best TV Show, Mike Read Best Radio Show and Boy George Prat of the Year. Ace!

5th February, 1985

I am a complete wreck. All this exam stress is getting me down. It's also playing havoc with me physically. My hair has gone greasy and it was only washed yesterday. I have also come out in a few spots which are giving me hell. You can't get chicken pox THREE times can you? And finally, I'm sure I've got fatter!

25th March

I'm not using Sherry Gold toner again. Flaming stuff, my hair has gone almost ginger!

5th April

Had dinner at a pub. It was a bit embarrassing because there was this sexy boy winning on a fruit machine. There was I trying to make a good impression with a bit of make-up, and there was Gran saying, "Ooh, look at the ducks!" She won't accept that I'm a young lady now, not a kid!

17th September

Tiffany said she had a flowery flying suit to wear to the disco. Ugh! We were all very two faced about it. Mandy arranged a signal that she would stick her fingers up if she didn't like the suit, but if she gave a thumbs up it meant she did. Got ready in my pastel blue flying suit, white accessories, make-up and white stilettos. Tiffany's suit wasn't as bad as I'd imagined, but I still didn't like it much. Her heels were the same height as mine, but Nina's were bigger (of course). Got to the disco. When Tiffany wasn't looking, Mandy stuck her fingers up. Ha, ha!

4th October

When I got home, I found that Mum and Dad are buying a trendy washing machine to replace our old top loader one. ACE! I've wanted one for ages, ever since that Quartz advert. I think that Dad has won the Pools or something. He is now going on about buying a microwave! I am keeping my fingers crossed for one of those new video things. Well, you never know.

2nd November

Sandy and I found some great fuchsia pink blouses in Top Shop. They were £9.99, so that worked out well. They will go with the black dungarees I am getting from Tiffany's catalogue (which are 90p a week - hope Mum doesn't mind). I also bought some black and fuchsia earrings, which are ACE, and some fuchsia tights to go with it.

21st December

Diary should be well pleased tonight - I have given it a new coat! Well, to be exact, I've stuck on pics of everyone who's meant most to me and had been biggest in 1985. There are pics of Duran, Stephen Duffy, Boris Becker, Rik Mayall, Damon from Brookside, Ali from EastEnders, Les Dennis, Ghostbusters, Rainbow, Billy Bragg, Go West, Andrew Ridgeley, Nik Kershaw, Prince, John Nettles, Bob Geldof. There are also a few cut-outs like a Young Ones episode from Radio Times, words like 'Macbeth', 'Charlie Wolf', 'Laser 558', 'Men's Singles Winner: Boris Becker', '1999 – Prince' 'Into the Groove' sleeve, a Smash Hits cover, a photo of the German exchange people including Ralf, a cat sticker and in the middle, outlined to make it stand out, a picture of the Laser 558 boat MV Communicator along with a pic of Charlie, which gives them their pedestal as THE best thing in 1985 (although Germany was pretty close, of course).

Anyway, enough reminiscing!

***

The Untrendy Teenager began to publish excerpts from her 80's diaries online on her blog, My Secret 80s Diary, in early 2016. Using the pseudonym Lynette "to protect the innocent (and the guilty)", she perfectly captured the jumble of angst, awkwardness, obsession and fun of what it was like to be a teenager in the decade. However, only weeks after first publishing her blog, the bubbly mother-of-two unexpectedly passed away. It is with great sadness that I can now reveal The Untrendy Teenager's true identity as friend and fellow 80's fanatic, Cat Dodsworth. Her contributions to this publication have been included, as arranged prior to her passing, with the kind permission of her husband Martyn. Through them, may she continue to entertain and sparkle as she did in life.

***

Cat Dodsworth
in the 80s (top) and in 2016

Thanks for the Memories...

For many of us, the year began on a sad note, having lost The Specials' John Bradbury and Motörhead's Lemmy at the end of 2015. We were only a few days into January, when it became apparent that 2016 looked set to continue to take away those who had been an integral part of our childhood and adolescence. Here, we look back on the first four months of the year, when it felt as if we were losing a disproportionate number of those personalities, who left us with some fantastic and long-lasting memories.

****

January

9th - DJ and former Crackerjack and Top of The Pops presenter Ed 'Stewpot' Stewart died, aged 74, following a stroke.

10th - The world was in shock at the news of David Bowie's death, two days after his 69th birthday. The singer had kept private his battle with liver cancer, choosing instead to relay his struggle with the disease and his own mortality through his final studio album 'Black Star'. Debuting at No. 1, his final offering spent a further 12 weeks inside the Top 40, alongside a number of his previous recordings including re-releases of 'The Man Who Sold The World' and 'Scary Monsters'.

14th - He charmed his way onto our screens in 1988 as Die Hard's villainous Hans Gruber, yet Alan Rickman's rich, hypnotic tones had delighted our ears, albeit in a dodgy Greek accent, as early as 1985, when he played the character of Dimitri in the comedy series 'Girls On Top'. The actor was 69 when he lost his battle with pancreatic cancer.

18th - Lead singer with the Eagles, Glenn Frey is perhaps best remembered by the 80's generation as the man who brought us the 1985 hit, 'The Heat Is On'. The singer died following medical complications, whilst recovering from gastric surgery, aged 67.

26th - Colin Vearncombe, who released the 80's albums 'Wonderful Life' and 'Comedy' under the name Black, had sustained serious injuries earlier in the month when his vehicle was involved in a road traffic accident in Ireland. In a coma for over two weeks, the singer never regained consciousness, and passed away aged 53. His memorial service was held the following month at the Anglican Cathedral in Colin's native Liverpool.

31st - A reassuringly familiar sight and sound on TV and radio throughout

Alan Rickman

our youth, Terry Wogan died from cancer, aged 77.

****

February

3rd - Founder of the soul trio Earth, Wind & Fire, Maurice White died age 74, following a long struggle against Parkinson's Disease.

15th - Born Denise Matthews, the singer and actress better known as Vanity became synonymous with Prince, after he asked her to front the girl band Vanity 6. An addiction to crack cocaine resulted in her receiving a kidney transplant in 1994. She continued to undergo daily peritoneal dialysis, complications of which led to her death at the age of 57.

28th - George Kennedy, the actor behind Naked Gun's Captain Hocken and Carter McKay in Dallas, died of heart disease, aged 91.

****

March

6th - America's First Lady from 1981 to 1989, and hostess to the cast of Grange Hill, Nancy Reagan suffered heart failure at the age of 94.

10th - Most noted for his work with Emerson, Lake & Palmer, Keith Emerson committed suicide, aged 72, by shooting himself in the head.

17th - Magician Paul Daniels, who repeatedly assured us we'd "like it, but not a lot" died of a brain tumour, aged 77.

22nd - Malik Taylor, better known as Tribe Called Quest's Phife Dawg died from diabetes related complications, aged 45.

31st - The smaller half of The Two Ronnies, and Timothy Lumsden in the BBC comedy 'Sorry', Ronnie Corbett died from motor neurone disease at the age of 85.

****

April

13th - Gareth Thomas, who played the eponymous character in the space series Blake's 7, suffered heart failure, aged 71.

Gareth Thomas

20th - BAFTA winning comedian and actress Victoria Wood died from cancer, following a year-long private battle with the disease, at the age of 62.

21st - Fans across the globe were stunned by the announcement that Prince had passed away. Only days beforehand, the diminutive star's plane had been force to make an emergency landing in Illinois, when the singer had been taken ill. Subsequent reports stated that his Royal Purpleness had been discharged from hospital, and he had been feeling unwell due to a bout of flu the previous week.

The news of Prince's death, later revealed to have been caused by an accidental overdose of the prescription drug Fentanyl, therefore came as a huge shock. His domination of the charts in the mid-Eighties, epitomised by the eight week run inside the Top 20 by 'When Doves Cry', in the summer of '84, meant a generation of 40-somethings were left mourning not only a modern day music legend, but an intrinsic piece of their youth.

Victoria Wood

1989

That was the year...

The Sky was the limit

Sky TV became the UK's first satellite television service when it began broadcasting on 5th February.

****

Dirty Den's departure

In an episode watched by more than 20 million viewers, Leslie Grantham's character left EastEnders with a bang, when he was shot and fell into Walford Canal. In 2003, it was revealed that Den Watts had not died in the shooting, when he returned to the BBC soap.

****

Nigel Mansell stepped up a gear

Making his debut for Ferrari, the British racing driver won the Brazilian Grand Prix on 26th March. His victory in the first race of the Formula One season saw Mansell become the first competitor to win a race in a car with a semi-automatic gearbox.

****

Hillsborough Disaster

Tragedy struck during the FA Cup semi-final match between Liverpool and Nottingham Forest on 15th April, when the Leppings Lane stand at the Sheffield Wednesday football ground became dangerously overcrowded, and spectators became trapped. The ensuing crush resulted in the deaths of 96 Liverpool fans. A further 766 people were injured.

****

Tiananmen Square Massacre

Protests began at the Beijing landmark on 15th April, following the death of former head of the Communist Party of China, Hu Yaobang. Demonstrations continued throughout the next six weeks, with the number of protesters growing and reaction by the Chinese government becoming increasingly aggressive. By the evening of 4th June, tanks of government troops had entered the capital to forcibly remove anyone in the square. Although unconfirmed by the Chinese authorities, it is thought up to 1,000 people died and 7,000 were injured as the country took back control from its people.

****

Timothy Dalton lost his Bond

Released in the UK on 4th August, Licence To Kill was the Welsh actor's second and final appearance in the role of James Bond.

****

The Berlin Wall Fell

On 9th November, East Germany announced its border with West Germany, which had been closed since 1961, could be crossed freely. The following celebrations saw Germans from both sides partying together on and around the formerly dividing wall.

****

Iliescu deposed Ceauşescu

The deposition on 22nd December brought Romania's communist regime to an end. Three days later, on Christmas Day, Nicolae Ceauşescu and his wife Elena were executed by the new Romanian government.

****

We said a final goodbye to:

Bette Davis, Don Revie, Graham Chapman, Irving Berlin, Laurence Olivier, Laurie Cunningham, Salvador Dali and Sugar Ray Robinson.

****

UK Chart Toppers included:

Soul II Soul
- Back To Life

Black Box
- Ride On Time

Marc Almond & Gene Pitney
- Something's Gotten Hold of My Heart

Jason Donovan
- Too Many Broken Hearts and Sealed With A Kiss

Madonna
- Like A Prayer
Bangles
- Eternal Flame.

****

Top Films of the Year included:

Shirley Valentine,
Scandal, Look Who's Talking,
Born on the Fourth of July,
Bill & Ted's Excellent
Adventure, Batman,
Driving Miss Daisy,
When Harry Met Sally,
Dead Poet's Society,
My Left Foot,
Tango & Cash,
Uncle Buck, and
See No Evil, Hear No Evil.

****

Rear of The Year:

There was no competition this year, but had there been, Joanne Whalley would have been a hot favourite in the judging.

95

We're All Grown Up

Dancing and singing along as Hazel O'Connor performed 'Eighth Day' and 'D-Days', I found myself overwhelmed with elation as the lights dimmed, a solitary spotlight focussed on the singer, and she delivered a sublime rendition of 'Will You?'. It was thirty years since I had received her handwritten response to my teenage request for her help with a book I was writing, and for three decades I had cherished that response. Now, I am in a position where I can share our correspondence.

****

My letter (including incorrect grammar and punctuation) read:

"Dear Hazel,

Please could you help me with a book I'm trying to write by writing and telling me your 5 favourite songs of all time. Some photo's of yourself that could be printed in the book would also be appreciated. I'd be grateful if you could fill in the questionnaire I've enclosed & send it to me so I could do a fact file on you in the book.

Thanking you in anticipation. I look forward to hearing from you. All the best for the future.

**Yours sincerely,
Sarah Lewis."**

These were her answers to the questions I posed in 1985.

Date of Birth: 16.5.55
Place of Birth: Coventry
Colour of Hair: Blonde
Colour of Eyes: Blue
Height: 5' 4"
Pets: Dogs

Favourite Drink:
Chocolate milk, Perrier water

Favourite Food:
Vegetarian curry

Favourite Actor:
Harrison Ford

Favourite Actress:
Glenda Jackson

Favourite Singer:
Edith Piaf

Ambition:
To be happy

Likes:
Big heartedness

Dislikes:
Liars, cheats

Wishes:
At present, new car!

Who would you most like to meet: Bogart

Five favourite songs:
Small Faces - Itchycoo Park

Ultravox - Vienna

Eurythmics - Sweet Dreams

Stranglers - No More Heroes

Bob Marley - No Woman, No Cry

80's SINGERS WORDSEARCH

```
X N S V B P W E D B E S T S G L V T L G
Y O G I D K P H O Y E D H G X W A N P E
L W N K M L X Y I N M A L V W D T A I O
N P R N R O G J O T K J R I S B S M W R
O U R C E E N J W I N A E G W P R A B G
T A Y I O L D L N F N E L Y A M C D I E
O B R R N R E S E N L V Y J L P I A M M
N I G D A C T I O B A U T H W G L K K I
Y E S W F E E D N S O O E N O Y W Y Z C
H A O N V P A M O N J N I G J U Q A U H
A H N E C M D C X I A S N Z P I S R N A
D A N I K K E R S H A W N G R N H T X E
L S F G B V Z P J G I E O U L G Z D O L
E R I Z V S C I C F R L B E A P S M W N
Y U C S F Z G M J F S T X V M C J I S N
A V V J E R S O I F G Z D T B H Y D Q V
G D J R U J H J G N U O Y L U A P M G U
N O S N H O J Y L L O H J C P N F N V V
M I C H A E L J A C K S O N O Z C C S Y
G R H V D T I F F A N Y S F D G P X X N
```

Adam Ant	**Howard Jones**	**Prince**
Annie Lennox	**Kim Wilde**	**Shakin' Stevens**
Bonnie Tyler	**Madonna**	**Simon Le Bon**
Boy George	**Michael Jackson**	**Tiffany**
George Michael	**Nik Kershaw**	**Tony Hadley**
Holly Johnson	**Paul Young**	**Whitney Houston**

Answers at back of book

Me, Myself and I

Me dressed as Boy George in 1982

Backstage with Immaculate Fools' Andy Ross, after my first gig in 1985

With Kevin Godley in 1986

With Bob Geldof in 1988

Road trip in my Allegro in 1989

With Buster Bloodvessel

Now you've reached the end of The 80's Annual, some of you may be wondering who is this Sarah Lewis and why did she put this book together? The short answer is - a huge fan of the Eighties, who wanted to revive and share some of the fun and frivolity from that time. I was still in single figures when the decade of change began, and reached adulthood at the beginning of 1989, so the Eighties also represent a very personal period of transition for me.

****

From wearing a sailor top and ra-ra skirt at my primary school disco to sporting a satin and velvet peplum dress with gigantic shoulder pads the first time I went nightclubbing, I loved and embraced the fashions (although, looking at some of the outfits I wore, I don't think they loved me back!) with

a fervour like none I have experienced since. I would spend hours copying the hair and make-up of those I had seen performing on Top of The Pops, in magazines or on record sleeves. Toyah, Boy George and the girl on the cover of Wham!'s 'Wake Me Up Before You Go Go' single were just some of those I attempted to imitate, before settling on my own individual "style" in the mid-Eighties - pearlescent pink eyeshadow, electric blue eyeliner and mascara, Bon Bon lipstick and a change of hair colour every other week!

My appearance may have varied throughout the Eighties, but one thing that remained constant was my love of music. Every day, I am amazed at how that passion continues to manifest itself in the unearthing of long forgotten memories of yesteryear. Eurythmics' 'Who's That Girl' plays and I'm suddenly in a caravan in Burnham-on-Sea, during the long, hot summer of 1983; each

time Owen Paul's 'My Favourite Waste of Time' comes on the radio, I think of the penfriend I made during the summer of '86, courtesy of Smash Hits magazine; Inner City's 'Good Life' will always be the first road trip I made in my Austin Allegro, having taken my A level exams in 1989. Such is the incredible power of music, I feel it is a real privilege every time I meet those involved in the songs of my youth, and interview them for my various writing projects. It is why I write as a fan, not a critic or "expert".

****

Currently, I am working on my third book on 80's popular culture 'More Eighties', which is due to be published in 2017. My website www.my-eighties.co.uk features details about my other publications, 'My Eighties' and 'Your Eighties', and other information such as my blog and social media. Twitter is where you'll often find me (t)wittering away, so come and tweet me @MyEighties.

With Ranking Roger

With Musical Youth's Michael Grant and Dennis Seaton

With Martin Fry

With Nathan Moore

With Londonbeat

With Leo Sayer

Solutions and Acknowledgements

80's Fashion Word Search

```
V T U F J T R P Y V S J C P M N  B S P W
S M R U I I A B W H Z O R I K B A T E L
S V B I A N K R E B R Z N X D T T N M O
C Z U H H F G L T K W E X I S S W A S U
X I G T X S L E S A D H M E S N I P R M
T I U H S S T C R E N H L B M O N I B S
B R H C U I R N L L C F F O A O G K I E
R H N I A E A B A I E L Y O E D S S Y L
X C T J W L U W K G L S Y T Z O L E H L
J S D P O O E G H N O Z S S M I E V Q I
W E G D E E G T G O L B G O E X M R
Y R M U L L E T W Z I U S X L M V Z A D
M V T R I K S A R A R H J S Z O E T Q A
I I K L O W M P L L R C B I J B V C P P
C Y L T W V P E X U T M W S D P Z E R S
O O N W S H Y B Z H Y E E I Z R W X S E
S D A P R E D L U O H S U R D E E Q U U
F R I L L Y S H I R T Y T L S G I J M R
Y G B L K X A G I J M Q Z D G K V K A L
Z O C V W S I H K W D N B X Y G P I W F
```

80's Singers Word Search

```
X N S V B P W E D B E S T S G L V T L G
Y O G I D K P H O Y E D H G X W A N P E
L W N K M L X Y I N M A L V W D T A I O
N P R N R O G J O T K J R I S B S M W R
O U R C E E N J W I N A E G W P R A B G
T A Y I O L D L N F N E L Y A M C D I E
O B R R N R E S E N L V Y J L P I A M M
N I G D A C T I O B A U T H W G L K K I
Y E S W F E E D N S O O E N O Y W Y Z C
H A O N V P A M O N J N I G J U Q A U H
A H N E C M D C X I A S N Z P I S R N A
D A N I K K E R S H A W N G R N H T X E
L S F G B V Z P J G I E O U L G Z D O L
E R I Z V S C I C F R L B E A P S M W N
Y U C S F Z G M J F S T X V M C J I S N
A V V J E R S O I F G Z D T B H Y D Q V
G D J R U J H J G N U O Y L U A P M G U
N O S N H O J Y L L O H J C P N F N V V
M I C H A E L J A C K S O N O Z C C S Y
G R H V D T I F F A N Y S F D G P X X N
```

80's Music Crossword

Across:
1. The 2. Razzmatazz 7. Free 11. Elton John 14. Paul Young 15. Do 16. Sleep 17. All 18. Uno 19. TL (To Live) 20. Do 22. Mod 23. F.L.M. 24. Monday 27. O'Jays 29. Toy 30. Na Na 31. Oh 32. AD (And Die) 34. TH (Terry Hall) 35. Hi 36. Mandela 38. Cry 39. Club 40. Bad 41. La 43. Mask 44. Palmas Seven 49. Pure 50. Mall 53. Fidelity 54. Ant

Down:
1. Temptation 2. Return Of The Los 3. Zang Tuum Tumb 4. Moon 5. Al 6. ZZ Top 8. Reynolds 9. E.L.O. 10. Hull 12. On 13. Nelson 15. De 19. Toyah 20. Do 21. La 22. Man 24. My 25. DJ 26. Yah 28. Jarreau 32. Adam 33. De Da Da 34. Talk 37. NB (Nick Beggs) 42. Da 44. P.P. 45. LR (Linda Ronstadt) 46. Me 47. Eve 48. EMI 50. My 51. La 52. LN (Les Nemes)

Everything 80s Crossword

Across:
2. Ren McCormack 8. Spurs 10. AS (Ayrton Senna) 12. Cop 13. Obsession 16. HT (Helen Terry) 17. Jazz 19. Bikes 20. Repo 21. BAE (Bert and Ernie) 22. Flo 23. OC 25. Well 26. ETE (Eddie The Eagle) 29. Love 31. EM (Ennio Morricone) 33. In 35. Deely Boppers 37. The 38. AAO (Against All Odds) 39. Jo 40. Space Dust 42. Sam 44. C.A.T.S. Eyes 46. Owner 49. Doh! 50. SL (Stephanie Lawrence) 51. KLF 54. YSL 56. Maggie Forbes 60. Owen 62. DF (Dexter Fletcher) 63. CH (Coco Hernandez) 64. Superstore

Down: 1. Spot 2. RR (Roger Rabbit) 3. Escape 4. My 5. Cabbage Patch Kids 6. Ossie 7. Muse 8. School Disco 9. Up 11. Snood 14. EK (Eddie Kidd) 15. SS (Steve Strange) 17. Jewel 18. Zola Budd 24. Coe 27. Tiswas 28. En 30. Vega   32. Meo 34. Rhodes 36. PAS (Pepsi and Shirley) 37. TJ 41. Cue 42. Stiff 43. Met 45. Slush

****

47. Nile 48. Rum 49. Dog 52. Left 53. CB 54. Yo
55. SWW (Slippery When Wet) 57. Amp 58. Rae
59. 'Eck 61. NS (Nu Shooz)

****

Quizzing Times:

1. 50 (5 x 10) 2. 250 (1000 ÷ 4) 3. 6,000 (3 x 2,000) 4. 9
(45 ÷ 5) 5. 14 (7 x 2) 6. 61 (19 + 42) 7. 0 (4 - 4) 8. 33 (12
+ 21) 9. 71 (73 - 2) 10. 563 (5 + 558)

****

Lyrically Challenged:

1. Wham! - Last Christmas 2. Tight Fit - Fantasy Island
3. Level 42 - Running In The Family 4. The Jam - Eton
Rifles 5. Adam & The Ants - Prince Charming 6. De La
Soul - Eye Know 7. The Specials - Gangsters 8. Dire
Straits - Brothers In Arms 9. Iron Maiden - Run To The
Hills 10. Bros - Drop The Boy 11. Madonna - Crazy For
You 12. Scritti Politti - Wood Beez (Pray Like Aretha
Franklin) 13. Prefab Sprout - King of Rock 'n' Roll
14. Neneh Cherry - Manchild 15. Madness - Cardiac
Arrest 16. Deacon Blue - Dignity 17. Dexys Midnight
Runners - Geno 18. Bronski Beat - Small Town Boy
19. The Police - Don't Stand So Close To Me
20. Lisa Stansfield - Around The World 21. Bucks Fizz -
Land of Make Believe 22. Duran Duran - Union of the
Snake 23. Meat Loaf - Dead Ringer For Love 24. Prince -
Raspberry Beret 25. Culture Club - Victims

****

Pop Quiz:

1. Where Did Your Heart Go 2. 19 3. Red Red Wine -
UB40, Lady in Red - Chris de Burgh, 99 Red Balloons -
Nena 4. Simple Minds 5. Shelley Preston 6. Delroy 7. Dr
Robert 8. Department S 9. Van Morrison 10. Siouxsie &
The Banshees 11. Dazz Band 12. Jo Boxers 13. 16 14.
Iko Iko 15. Each features a harmonica solo by Stevie
Wonder 16. Phil Collins (86 & 89) 17. Mad World Tears for
Fears 18. Gladys Knight 19. The Jam (Going
Underground /Dreams of Children) 20. A Little Peace by
Nicole 21. Lil Louis 22. A Different Corner by George
Michael 23. London Calling by The Clash (even though it
was released in 1979) 24. The Cure 25. In Too Deep 26.
Crazy For You 27. Kylie Minogue 28. Judas Priest 29.
Love Train 30. Mirror In The Bathroom by The Beat

****

Who's That Boy?:

Neville Staple
(Fun Boy Three and The Specials)

Acknowledgements:

Alan Read, Alex Dyke, Andy Kyriacou,
Ariel Hyatt, Ben Watson, Bruce Foxton,
Cat Dodsworth, Christine Staple,
Clark Datchler, Clive Jackson,
Dave Brewis, Dave Meadows,
Dennis Seaton, Dougie Trendle,
Feena Quinn, Gaps Hendrickson,
Garry Bushell, Gerda De Haan,
Guy Helliker, Harriet Armstrong
Photography, Hazel O'Connor,
Hazell Dean, Ian Donaldson,
Jamie Emmott, Jamie Moses,
Jay Aston, Jeff Cox, Jill Bryson,
Jimmy Helms, Jo Bartlett, John Parr,
John Smith, Mandy Taylor-Slangewal,
Mark Shaw, Mark Taylor,
Marnie Richards, Martin Fry,
Martyn Dodsworth, Matthew Rudd,
Michael Eccleshall, Nathan Moore,
Neville Staple, Nick Beggs,
Owen Paul, Paul Hardcastle,
Pauline Black, Pete Cunliffe,
Phil Fearon, Richard Coles,
Russell Hastings, Sarah Moss,
Steve Blacknell, Steve Haywood,
Sylvia Bell, Tanya Raftery,
Teddie Dahlin, Valerie Day.

****

Fairground Attraction photo shoot:

Alan Langley Photography,
Dreamland Margate:
Milly Maxwell-Scott,
Madam Popoff Vintage Emporium:
Deborah Ellis,
Hair: Hayley Edwards,
Make-Up Artist: Nina Gregory,
Models: Mason Mellor, Oli Stevens,
Robyn Gillian Daisy Lamont, Sophie
Price.

Sarah Lewis

Sarah is a self-confessed obsessive of Eighties culture, and a mine of useless trivia on the decade. With an uncanny knack of bumping into celebrities, the ability to recall in startling detail events from over three decades ago (although likely to forget what she ate for breakfast!), and a number of diaries kept during her childhood and teenage years, no one is better placed to bring you a true taste of the Eighties.

Born and raised in The Garden of England, Sarah has lived in Kent all her life. Growing up surrounded by beautiful countryside, but miles from 'civilisation', saw her innate interest in music become a lifelong infatuation with radio and vinyl. Entrusted with her parents' record collection from a young age, she spent hours listening to an eclectic mix of songs from Jim Reeves to The Kinks, Elvis to Sam Cooke, Otis Redding to The Rolling Stones. The latter's "High Tide And Green Grass" album remains a firm favourite. At 10 years old, Sarah began her own vinyl collection when she bought her first 7" single in Woolworths, Adam & The Ants' "Stand & Deliver". Today, that now sizeable collection continues to grow with both new releases by 80's artists and old classics, found in charity shops or received as gifts from friends. Played whenever she feels like taking a break from the radio, her "daily default background music", Sarah believes her fascination with the Eighties has been compounded by years of exposure to its music, including gigs and retro festivals.

A desire to share her enthusiasm for the decade of her youth, and explore its appeal with fellow 80's fans led Sarah to set up her blog myeighties.wordpress.com. This was swiftly followed by her first printed publication on the time that subtlety forgot, My Eighties, which includes celebrity interviews alongside her own personal anecdotes and memories. Your Eighties continues the exploration of the decade of extremes, with an array of recollections from some of the era's biggest fans and best known faces. The third book in the trilogy, More Eighties, is currently a work in progress and will be released by New Haven Publishing in 2017.

Follow Sarah on Twitter @MyEighties
Facebook:
https://www.facebook.com/MyEightiesUK
Website: http://www.my-eighties.co.uk

CPSIA information can be obtained
at www.ICGtesting.com
Printed in the USA
LVOW02*1359211216

518283LV00005B/236/P

9 781910 705490